D1188101

Hard-Pressed
in the Heartland

Hard-Pressed
in the Heartland

The Hormel Strike
and the Future
of the Labor Movement

Peter Rachleff

South End Press
Boston, Massachusetts

Cover design by John Moss
Text design and production by South End Press
Printed by union labor in the U.S.A.
First edition, first printing

Library of Congress Cataloging-in-Publication Data

Rachleff, Peter J.
Hard-pressed in the heartland: the Hormel strike and the future of the labor movement / by Peter Rachleff.
p. cm.
Includes bibliographical references and index.
1. Geo. A Hormel & Company Strike, Austin, Minn., 1985-1986.
2. United Packinghouse, Food, and Allied Workers. Local 9 (Austin, Minn.) 3. Strikes and lockouts—Packing-house workers—Minnesota—Austin. I.Title.
HD5325.P152 1985.A877 1992 92-26022
331.89'28649'00977617—dc20 CIP
ISBN 0-89608-450-7: $12.00 (paper)
ISBN 0-89608-451-5: $30.00 (cloth)

South End Press, 116 Saint Botolph Street, Boston, MA 02115
TP   98 97 96 95 94 93   1 2 3 4 5 6 7 8 9

Dedicated to the Memory
of Jake Cooper, Harry DeBoer,
and Floyd Lenoch

Table of Contents

Acknowledgements

While I take responsibility for this book's conclusions, writing it would never have been possible without the contributions of many, many people. Countless P-9ers and their family members spoke with me, gave documents to me, and shared their experiences, fears, and hopes with me. They were more than sources of information; they were my teachers. I am aware that by mentioning any I risk overlooking some, but I must recognize my debt to Jim Guyette, Vicky Guyette, Pete Winkels, Lynn Houston, Dan Allen, Denny Mealy, Cecil Cain, Barb Collette, Skinny and Gloria Weiss, Floyd Lenoch, Merrill Evans, Merle and Madeline Krueger, Tom and Carol Keough, Pete Kennedy, Kathy Buck, Buck and John Heegard, Rod Huinker, Jim Getchell, Mike and Jeannie Bambrick, Jim and Carmine Rogers, and Dick Shattuck. Retirees like John Winkels and Paul Rasmussen, Hormel workers from other plants like Bob Langemeier of Fremont, and packinghouse activists from other employers like Janice Herritz of Oscar Meyer greatly added to my understanding of the depth and breadth of this struggle. So did Ray Rogers, Ed Allen, Phil Mattera, and Hardy Green of Corporate Campaign, Inc. Several attorneys—Rick MacPherson, Peggy Winters, Emily Bass, Ken Tilsen, and Joe Vass—shared extensive documents and their insights with me.

Labor activists in the Twin Cities Support Committee also helped me understand what was happening. Bud Schulte taught me volumes about meatpacking and about what a militant union presence on the shopfloor was all about. Dave Riehle shared his rich knowledge of the Minnesota labor movement and his perceptive insights about how to keep a movement moving forward. Tom Laney taught me that "an injury to one is an injury to all" can actually be the motivating watchword of a union activist's daily life. Jake Cooper taught me to "never put the period to anyone," that everyone has the capacity to change. Harry DeBoer hammered home the connection between union democracy and rank-and-file militancy. My thinking about the strike and about the capacities of rank-and-file workers was strongly influenced by conversations I had with such support committee members as Gladys MacKenzie, Sal Salerno, Pat Claflin, Kevin O'Keefe, Dick Mitchell, Tom Dvorak, Al Gulden, Doug and Colleen McGilp, Bill Bader, Bernie Hesse, Joel Carr, Jim Gehres, John Sielaff, Larry Dunham, Dennis and Mary Jones, Randy and Gillian Furst, Ted LeValley,

1

and Melanie Benson. Larry Long, Sal Salerno, Paula Williamson, Chris Spotted Eagle, and Paul Metsa helped me understand the vital role of the arts in a revival of the labor movement. P-9 supporters from outside the Twin Cities—Gary Cox, Darrell Becker, Ron Wiesen, Jeff Crosby, General Baker, Pete Kelly, Brian Lang, Bill Henning, Dave Poklinkoski, Tony Mazzocchi, Jack Maloney, Al Netland, Paul Iverson, and Paul Pechter, among many—helped me understand the significance of this struggle to the labor movement as a whole.

Labor journalists Dick Blinn, Drew Mendelson, Jim Smoger, Barb Kucera, and Dexter Arnold added additional dimensions to my framework. In their book, *No Retreat, No Surrender,* Dave Hage and Paul Klauda provided valuable information on the strategies and behind-the-scenes activities of the Hormel Company, the United Food & Commerical Workers International Union, and the Minnesota State AFL-CIO. Hardy Green, a former member of the Corporate Campaign, Inc. staff, provided valuable information on the role of private detectives, the local and state police, the county sheriff's department, and the National Guard in his study *On Strike at Hormel.* He also helped me get a copy of the file the Austin police department kept on me.

Several other people helped this project along in different ways. David Montgomery, Jeremy Brecher, Staughton Lynd, Stan Weir, and the late George Rawick influenced my thinking about the labor movement in countless ways. Weir, Brecher, and David Roediger encouraged me to produce a book on this struggle. Steve Chase, my editor at South End Press, encouraged me to see the project through and provided several helpful editorial suggestions which improved the manuscript. Roger Horowitz and Rick Halpern shared with me their rich oral history interviews about the history of meatpacking unionism, as well as their own insights about the development of the union in the 1930s. Kim Moody, Jim Woodward, and Phill Kwik from *Labor Notes* provided intelligent sounding-boards for my ideas and also contributed ideas and analyses of their own. My wife, Meg, shared the joys and pains of these events with me, offered her own analyses of them, and kept me solidly grounded.

The Truth Left
on the Cutting Room Floor

The 1980s was arguably the bleakest decade in the entire history of the U.S. labor movement. Unions, declining in both size and influence, lost more organizing campaigns than they won. They appeared powerless to resist corporate decisions to close factories and eliminate jobs. Union workers were forced to make concessions, their wages falling behind not only inflation, but even, in some cases, behind non-union workers. Strikes were broken and strikers were permanently replaced. Across America, the rich grew richer, the middle class shrank, and the poor grew poorer.

For many commentators who bemoaned these developments, the Hormel Strike of 1985-86 came to symbolize this disaster. Seventeen hundred workers, employed in a modern, state-of-the-art plant by a profitable corporation untouched by foreign competition, were backed against a wall. Their refusal to knuckle under to their employer's demands for concessions led to a prolonged strike. When Hormel chose to reopen five months into the strike and the governor of Minnesota provided the services of the National Guard, 460 union members crossed their own picket lines, joining 550 newly hired "permanent replacements." Faithful union members lost their jobs. In time, many lost their cars, their homes, and even their marriages.

This is all some commentators see. They place the blame on a greedy corporate management and an anti-union political climate. Some even blame the local union leadership for embarking on a "suicide mission." Many commentators look for solutions in the election of Democrats, the passage of legislation limiting the use of "permanent replacements," and the bolstering of American "competitiveness" vis-à-vis Japan and other foreign economic powers.

3

But the Hormel Strike was more than symbolic of labor's decline in the 1980s. Contrary to the pessimism of many commentators, the heartbreaking struggle against Hormel's draconian concession demands powerfully suggests how to revitalize a militant, rank-and-file, labor movement that goes well beyond the bureaucratic "business unionism" that has so dominated organized labor since World War II. The Hormel Strike, while failing to achieve its specific goals, highlights several promising organizational and strategic approaches that will be necessary if the U.S. labor movement is ever to recover, let alone spearhead the creation of a humane, democratic economy. I am convinced that by better understanding the roots of this struggle and what actually happened in Austin, labor activists and their supporters around the country might be better prepared to tackle their own local situations and the deepening crisis in the American labor movement. Here is one story that proves that working people can be powerful agents for social change.

My purpose in writing this book is to make sure these lessons are not lost to labor's rank-and-file and other social justice activists. This is more urgent now than ever since the release of *American Dream,* Barbara Koppel's 1991 Academy Award-winning documentary about the Hormel Strike. This "critically acclaimed" movie has done something to the members of Local P-9 and their supporters that the Hormel Company, the United Food & Commercial Workers Union (UFCW), and the Minnesota National Guard could never do—turn them into "hapless victims." Granted, the P-9ers lost their strike, their jobs, and their union. But while they were victimized, they were never victims, something completely lost in Koppel's documentary.

What moved thousands upon thousands of P-9 supporters was not the strikers' victimization. What fired imaginations from one corner of this country to another was their living, breathing vision of a participatory, democratically-controlled union creatively fighting concessions. Local P-9 had gone from an apathetic union, like so many others—lucky to get a quorum at a monthly meeting—to a union—unlike almost all others—lucky to find a meeting room big enough to hold those who wanted to attend. The excitement this generated led 3,000 local unions to send aid to P-9. It also sparked the support of farm activists, peace and justice activists, Native American activists, and thousands of others, who saw their hopes reflected in this struggle. Every bit of this material ended up on Barbara Koppel's cutting room floor.

At the same time, *American Dream* presents the International Union's hatchet man, Lewie Anderson, as a tough-talking, hard-nosed union bargainer in contrast to P-9's leadership and advisers who are presented as confused, inexperienced, and out of touch with reality. Worse than these character distortions, *American Dream* also gives Anderson one opportunity after another to predict that this strike will fail, without ever exploring the critical role he and the UFCW played in undermining it—in discouraging other unions from sending assistance, in denying P-9 the right to block production at Hormel's seven other unionized plants, in rejecting P-9's call for a boycott of Hormel products, and in organizing a minority of dissident P-9 members to disrupt union meetings and even to cross sanctioned picket lines. *American Dream* actually implies that the UFCW had the "right" position—not to take on Hormel at all, or to return to work on the company's terms when they began to hire "permanent replacements"—at the same time it whitewashes the union's role in destroying a strike it publicly claimed to support.

My very different perspective on the strike is informed by my active participation in the P-9 support effort. When, in the summer of 1982, I moved from New England to Minnesota to take a teaching position in U.S. History at Macalester College in St. Paul, I quickly got involved with the informal strike support network there. In the fall of 1984, a number of us drove to Austin for a rally organized by Local P-9. We had little idea what to expect, and we were amazed by what we found—the large numbers of people participating, the involvement of families, the spirit and imagination that infused the event, and the determination not to back down before what appeared to be unreasonable demands being made by a profitable company. This struck me as just what the doctor ordered as an antidote for a moribund labor movement.

Over the next year, I became more involved in strike support for P-9, especially after their leadership asked our loose network to formally organize a Twin Cities P-9 Support Committee. We participated in some informational picketing and tried to expand the network of sympathetic labor activists by arranging for speakers from P-9 to visit local unions' regular meetings. Our committee grew in size, from a core of 25 or so, to a network of more than 100. We began holding regular meetings of our own.

In the summer of 1985, I was elected chair of this committee. Being a historian, I also collected copies of all leaflets, news articles, buttons, and paraphenalia. My wife accused me of having an entire dresser drawer full of P-9 T-shirts, most of which didn't even fit. I also kept minutes of our support committee meetings. Most of these materials have been turned over to the Minnesota Historical Society, where anyone who is interested can consult them. More importantly, I took part in numerous meetings with P-9 activists, got to know their leadership, and had many opportunities for extensive interviews. Since so much of my information comes from these sources, I have chosen not to use footnotes in this text. I have provided a bibliography for interested readers.

By actively participating in this struggle, I was able to see first hand the distorting gaps in Koppel's vision. As a historian, I felt I could bring this missing story to life, building on the articles I wrote about the strike in the late 1980s for *Labor Notes, Socialist Review,* and *Z Magazine,* as well as the essay I wrote for *Building Bridges: The Emerging Grassroots Coalition of Labor & Community,* edited by Jeremy Brecher and Tim Costello.

The book you are about to read will take you into different dimensions of this struggle—recent labor/management history; the importance of P-9's legacy in the Independent Union of All Workers; the efforts of Jim Guyette and the activists around him to rescue P-9 from the morass of business unionism and revive it as an expression of democratic, rank-and-file unionism; the tremendous support their stand won them in the hearts and minds of frustrated rank-and-file trade unionists from every corner of the labor movement, and even from peace and justice, community, and environmental activists; the ferocious opposition this drew from all levels of the government, regardless of political affiliation, and from the leadership of the labor movement, inside and outside the UFCW. Finally, the last chapter will focus on the strategic "lessons" from this struggle, particularly for those hearty souls, who either by choice or necessity, are committed to "putting the movement back in the labor movement."

This last chapter may seem strange coming from someone who gets paid to study the past. Yet, as I have always told my students, I became a historian because I was interested in the future. *Hard-Pressed in the Heartland* gives me an opportunity to practice what I preach.

Part I

Roots of a Labor War

Chapter 1

U.S. Labor in the 1980s

Over the course of the 1980s, organized labor became a shrinking island in the sea of the U.S. workforce. In 1980, some 24 million workers belonged to unions, about 22 percent of those eligible. By 1986, unions had fallen to a little more than 17 million members, down to 18 percent of the workforce. Though the absolute decline levelled off in the late 1980s, the percentage continued to fall, sinking to 16 percent in 1990. Among those employed in the private sector, only 10 percent are still covered by union contracts. By 1990, the percentage of unionized workers in the United States ranked lower than Australia, Belgium, Canada, Denmark, France, West Germany, Italy, Japan, the Netherlands, Sweden, Switzerland, and the United Kingdom. It was also dropping faster than in any of these countries.

One important reason for the shrinking of labor's island was what some economists have called "deindustrialization." Over the course of the 1980s, millions of manufacturing jobs disappeared from the U.S. economy. Some of this loss was a result of technological innovation, but the lion's share was due to the closing of factories and the export of capital—and jobs—to the low-wage areas of the Third World. Most of these jobs had been held by unionized workers. In the lexicon of the 1980s, they became "dislocated" workers suitable for "retraining"— that is, to take one of the growing number of low-paying, non-union, service sector jobs. They got pushed off the island and into the sea of unorganized workers and the unemployed.

Another important reason labor's island continued to shrink was the labor movement's lack of success in organizing workers in the new service sector jobs. Roughly one union organizing campaign out of every two succeeded in a victorious election. But barely one out of every two electoral victories resulted in a bargained contract. In sum, only one-quarter of union organizing efforts led to formal recognition and a legitimate contract.

Increased employer resistance deserves much of the credit for this record. In the context of the Keynesian-influenced growth of the mid-1940s through the late 1960s, most large corporations had grudgingly accepted unions as part of the industrial relations scheme. But as economic growth slowed, profitability declined, and international competition intensified, corporate challenges to unions increased. By the early 1980s, they were buttressed by the emergence of a veritable industry of "management consultants" who preached the virtues of a "union-free environment." At the same time, the Republican-dominated executive branch of the U.S. government relaxed its enforcement of labor laws and actively strengthened the employers' hand.

Employer resistance revolved around three strategies—communication, intimidation, and stalling. The first principle of the "union-free environment" was to co-opt the "voice" function of unions, to give employees the idea that the boss would listen to them. This principle spawned a dazzling array of programs—quality circles, quality of work life programs, labor-management cooperation, employee involvement, the team concept—all of which were intended to give employees the opportunity to communicate with management, or at least the idea that they could. This management strategy was so effective that it also appeared in unionized settings, where it was used to undercut worker allegiance to unions.

The second principle—intimidation—was a lot less subtle. When confronted with a union organizing campaign, management came down hard on the activists. Many consultants carried a bag of "dirty tricks." Here is where lax government enforcement played an important role. Despite the "protections" of the National Labor Relations Act (Wagner Act) of 1935, workers known—or suspected—to be organizing a union were frequently fired. Employers were willing to pay the minimal fines that a slow-moving National Labor Relations Board (NLRB) might eventually assess against them in exchange for being able to intimidate their workforce during a union campaign. While the NLRB had the authority to impose union recognition in the case of blatant labor law violations, it refrained from doing so in almost every situation. Industrial relations researchers estimate that, over the course of the 1980s, 10,000 workers a year were fired illegally in precisely these situations. This sort of intimidation played a chilling role in most unions' efforts to expand their presence.

The third principle—stalling—was fall back strategy when, miraculously, a union won an election. While management was required by law to bargain "in good faith" with this union, failure to reach a contract within one year of the election meant the election results would be set aside. With the aid of their consultants, corporate management took advantage of this loophole. The law itself never defined "in good faith," and so management developed the skills of "surface bargaining," of sitting at the table and going through the motions effectively enough to satisfy an already pro-management National Labor Relations Board. A year later and—presto!—the results of the election were erased. Typically, this process also led to the attrition of pro-union workers who, seeing little likelihood of union success, became fed up and quit.

Management's three-pronged strategy certainly depended on the support of the federal government. Reagan, and later Bush, appointed men and women to the NLRB and its regional boards who were not inclined to vigorously enforce laws that defended the rights of unions. Similarly, their appointments to the Occupational Safety and Health Administration (OSHA) and the Environmental Protection Agency (EPA) shared their ideological distaste for government regulation and intervention, further strengthening management's hand. Over his eight years in office, Reagan also appointed some 10,000 federal judges, most of whom shared his anti-union, anti-regulation philosophy. Thus, corporate management could pursue its resistance to union expansion with little fear of government interference.

The entire system of labor relations functioned to dispense what Twin Cities folksinger Paul Metsa aptly called "slow justice." When American Linen Supply Company fired seven women in Hibbing, Minnesota, for exercising their legal right to strike in 1987, it would take more than four years for the NLRB to order their reinstatement and the federal courts to issue the necessary enforcement orders. Similar anecdotes could be recited from every corner of the United States. This "slow justice" not only wore down activists, it discouraged many would-be activists from ever taking risks themselves.

Non-union workers could see that conditions for unionized workers were deteriorating, and that their unions appeared ineffectual in protecting them. As one somewhat cynical friend put it, "Why do I need a union to negotiate a wage cut for me? I can do that just fine for myself." "Concessions" bargaining—give-backs and take-aways—became the order of the day. Unions struggled to "hold the line" at the status quo. Management demanded, and often received, wage freezes or outright deductions, lower wages for new hires (the so-called "two-tier" system), reduced vacation days, increased co-payments on health insurance, and pension and health insurance cuts for retirees. They also pursued "flexibility" in work rules, which often meant radical changes in job descriptions, gutting seniority systems, erasing "past practices," and disrupting work life. In key industries—auto, steel, meatpacking, and trucking—management succeeded in dissolving industry "patterns" and pitting individual locals against one another in a competitive war. The "winner" (i.e., the one who got the work, kept the plant open, etc.) was the one who gave up the most!

It is obvious by now that yielding to such management demands did not "save" jobs. In many cases, it increased management's access to liquid funds and even hastened relocations and runaways. The net result of concessions bargaining was increased authority for management personnel on the one hand, and an intensified workload and increased insecurity for most workers on the other. In short, unionized workers in the 1980s worked harder, got paid less for it, and looked forward to a very uncertain future.

In *The Overworked American*, Juliet Schor presents data demonstrating that the average American worker puts in one full month more per year now than he/she did 20 years ago. Even with this extra work, his/her real pay check falls short of its 20-year-old counterpart. Schor argues it would take six extra weeks of work just to regain 1973's standards. Furthermore, workplaces changed in such a way that a new sort of injury became epidemic—"cumulative trauma." Back injuries, wrist injuries, painful disabilities due to making the same motion over and over again put the lie to such platitudes as "quality of work life" or "ergonomics." Management's response to this epidemic was to label workers "lazy" and "malingerers" and to agitate in state level politics for reductions in workers' compensation benefits. For many unionized workers, this all too literally added insult to injury.

Nowhere was the decline in organized labor's influence more acutely experienced than at the workplace itself. Conditions didn't just become more dangerous; work itself became more intense. Some of the pressure came from the introduction of new technologies which, at the same time, increased the monetary value of what workers were held responsible for while it decreased their ability to control their immediate work environments. Some of the pressure also came from the new management approaches that were introduced—what some critics have called "running on yellow" (i.e., on the very margin of breakdown) or "management by stress."

Indeed, a veritable epidemic of stress swept American workplaces. When a major national insurance company conducted a survey in 1990, it found that 46 percent of its respondents reported feeling "highly stressed"; 62 percent reported "exhaustion"; 62 percent experienced "anger or anxiety"; 60 percent suffered from headaches; 45 percent from an inability to sleep; 38 percent from ulcers; and even 33 percent from "depression." These conditions characterized union and non-union workplaces alike.

If, angered by their treatment and determined to resist these trends, unionized workers chose to go on strike, they faced management's most powerful club of all—the right to hire "permanent replacements." While management had enjoyed this legal right since a 1938 Supreme Court decision, it had not been utilized until the 1980s. Emboldened by Ronald Reagan's firing of more than 11,000 air traffic controllers in the summer of 1981 and eager to play all their cards, management added this tactic to their labor relations repertoire. In highly publicized strikes—Brown and Sharpe in Rhode Island, Phelps Dodge in Arizona, Hormel in Minnesota, and Ravenswood in West Virginia—workers with 20 or 30 years seniority lost their jobs for having the temerity to go on strike. State governments, often run by Democrats, proved no more sympathetic than Reagan, as they provided the Minnesota State Police and National Guard necessary to bring scabs through union picket lines.

In short order, the number of strikes declined almost to the point of non-existence. In 1991, the Bureau of Labor Statistics reported only 40 major (more than 1,000 participants) strikes, compared to the 1970s average of 269 such strikes per year. Workers certainly knew that employers were willing to resort to the radical tactic of outright replacement. Seventy to 80 percent of the corporations responding to surveys conducted by the Bureau of National Affairs in the late 1980s reported that they would "consider" hiring permanent replacements if faced with a strike. Technological advances had undermined the value of their skills, no matter how long they had been on the job. Reagan's willingness to replace the air traffic controllers, risking the nation's air safety, further suggested that no one was "too skilled" to be replaced.

Meanwhile, farm foreclosures, factory closings, and economic hard times guaranteed that there would always be a large pool of hungry, unemployed men and women, desperate enough for work to cross a picket line. The federal government's manipulation of unemployment benefits helped swell their ranks. While 72 percent of the unemployed had been able to collect unemployment benefits during the recession of 1975-76, only 45 percent were so fortunate during the recession of 1982-83. Indeed, by the later 1980s, economists estimated that only 30-35 percent of the unemployed were eligible for benefits.

Organized labor's influence declined not only at the bargaining table and in the workplace. In the political arena, Republicans and Democrats alike blithely ignored the plight of working people. Despite the millions of dollars of COPE, CAP, and PAC funds which union leaders funnelled into politicians' coffers, not one significant piece of pro-labor legislation emerged from the federal government. The most dramatic example came in April 1991, when 230,000 workers went on strike against the country's eleven largest railroads. After only eighteen hours, the House voted 400 to 5 to send the strikers back to work. The Senate concurred by a "unanimous consent" motion introduced jointly by Orrin Hatch and Ted Kennedy. Not only did they order an end to the strike, but they imposed the draconian conditions recommended by a "presidential emergency board," condemning more than 30,000 rail workers to the unemployment lines and tens of thousands of others to a lifetime of irregular schedules. At the same time, Congress remained silent while rail management abandoned tens of thousands of miles of track and paid itself enormous salaries and bonuses.

Deregulation, privatization, and free trade became the watchwords—the "Holy Trinity," says David Morris of the St. Paul-based Institute for Local Self-Reliance—of national economic policy. Behind an ideological smokescreen of "supply-side economics," federal policies promoted the greatest transfer of wealth in U.S. history—from the poor and the middle class to the rich. Over the course of the decade, the after-tax incomes of the richest 1 percent of Americans rose 160 percent, while the after-tax incomes of the poorest 60 percent fell more than 10 percent.

State-level policies were little better. Whether Democrats or Republicans held the reins of power, taxes on corporations and the rich were reduced and social spending was slashed. Corporations whipsawed states into offering inducement packages for investment—tax abatements, bond-issue financing, and infrastructure development. And when unionized workers challenged corporate policies by hitting the bricks, governors—Democrats as well as Republicans—responded by providing the National Guard to bring "permanent replacements" safely through picket lines.

The 1980s was a disaster for unions, union members, and all working people. That much is clear. Management anti-unionism and government policies played an important role in the making of this disaster. But the story—and the responsibility—does not end there. Why were unions so ill-prepared for this assault, and why were they so ineffectual in resisting it? To find the answer, we need to begin with the very construction of the modern labor relations system in the late 1930s-1940s. This system began with the most dramatic turnaround in U.S. labor history, but it ended with the construction of a system that—ultimately—hamstrung the labor movement in the crisis of the 1980s.

Unions had declined throughout the 1920s and the early 1930s, almost to the point of disappearance. But then, despite an unemployment rate of nearly 30 percent, well-organized employers, injunction-granting judges, and picket-line-busting county sheriffs, the labor movement made its greatest gains ever, organizing nearly eight million additional workers. The next chapter will tell part of this story by presenting a case study of the Independent Union of All Workers (IUAW), the militant predecessor of Local P-9. But, for now, let's look at the overall picture.

Labor activists in the 1930s refashioned union structures. For the millions of unskilled and semi-skilled workers in mines, mills, and factories, the traditional craft structure of unions no longer made sense. New industrial unions sought to unite everyone who worked for the same employer and link all those who worked in the same industry, so that companies could not use wages as their basis for competition. In some cases, such as the IUAW, unions linked all workers in communities or regions, thereby strengthening all of them.

Inside workplaces, activists encouraged workers to tackle their problems collectively and directly. When workers had a problem or dispute with a supervisor, they'd stop work on the spot until the issue was resolved. Only then would they resume work. Even more often, workers resorted to slowdowns to get their point across in workplace disputes. Such tactics gave unions a strong workplace presence and gave rank-and-file workers ultimate responsibility for the quality of their own working conditions.

The new unions used strikes as their chief weapon—whether it was a matter of gaining recognition from an employer, gaining a wage increase, or addressing a workplace issue. Strikes were more effective than grievance procedures, negotiation, arbitration, or mediation. When workers found it necessary to go on strike, they often sat down in their workplace, rather than set up a picket line outside. They felt that management would hesitate to send in sheriffs' deputies, the police, or even the National Guard. This strategy also avoided conflict with unemployed workers who might be willing to cross picket lines to seek work.

The new unions also reached out directly to the unemployed. They helped them to organize and took up their issues. Unions demonstrated for unemployment benefits, for government job creation and for fairness in the allocation of those jobs. They made special efforts to retain members who had lost their jobs, charging them only token dues but keeping them involved in the union's activities.

Union organizers also realized that the industrial workforce was incredibly diverse. They published campaign literature in multiple languages, urged the celebration of varied ethnic cultures and opposed racism wherever it appeared. They drew union members' families into the movement through auxiliaries, and they addressed community as well as workplace issues. Labor activists promoted the practice of solidarity. They joined each others' picket lines. They supported strikers by raising funds and collecting food. They not only boosted others' morale through such efforts; they also deepened their own commitment.

Striking workers paid little heed to court injunctions. Some felt that the judges were biased, and therefore considered it legitimate to disobey their orders. Few had enough savings to worry about fines. Even the unions had so little in their treasuries that fines and court attachments were almost meaningless.

In many communities, activists encouraged the organization of labor-based political parties. Even without the existence of formal parties, union members ran for school board or city council. Even when these candidates failed, their involvement put pressure on mainstream politicians to take the labor movement's concerns seriously.

The internal workings of the new unions were another piece of this puzzle. Democracy and participation were the order of the day. In lively union meetings, workers debated local, national, and international issues, and union newspapers presented diverse points of view. In some situations—such as the IUAW—the union became the center of a "movement culture" that prepared participants for the transformation of society as a whole.

Union stewards collected dues directly from the members. Upon paying the monthly dues, a worker received a button. Those without the proper button were pressured by their workmates. Direct dues collection maintained an open channel of communication between the steward and the rank-and-file worker. It was when paying dues face-to-face that a worker was most likely to voice an opinion about how well the union was doing its job. The distance between the leadership and the rank-and-file was small. Many officers continued to work, and even full-time officials earned little more than the workers in the shop. They continued to share the same lifestyles and values, even if they disagreed on specific issues.

While the national and, at times, the state governments were somewhat sympathetic to the labor movement, the new unions rarely looked to the government to solve their problems for them. Rather, they looked to their own rank-and-file, and to the rank-and-file membership of other unions. However, within years of their dramatic emergence, these new industrial unions moved away from these formative experiences and took a new direction that would lay the basis for the disaster of the 1980s.

There were a variety of reasons for this shift in course—the economic collapse of the U.S. economy (what some call the "second trough" of the Great Depression) in late 1937-1938; the shift, especially at the state level, of the political climate in the later 1930s; the impact of the legal channels for unions created by the Wagner Act (upheld by the U.S. Supreme Court in 1937); the worsening sectarian conflict within the U.S. Left, particularly between the Communists and Trotskyists; the growing political strength of the Democratic Party's "New Deal Coalition," and the consequent weakening of third party options. In some cases, rank-and-file workers grew tired of crises and conflicts, and sought stability. In other cases, pressure from employers and the government played a role. The contemporary system of labor relations was taking shape, and the internal structure and life of unions, even new unions, were changing.

In this environment, the builders of the CIO unions placed a premium on securing their existence through a contractual agreement with employers. They sought to negotiate "pattern" agreements industry by industry. Such contracts were obviously to be negotiated at a national level, taking much of the bargaining responsibility out of the hands of local unions. And, while these unions certainly supported each other across industry lines—through central labor bodies and industrial union councils—there was no room for essentially "horizontal" formations like the Independent Union of All Workers, which placed solidarity ahead of contractual relations with single employers. Indeed, the new unions' primary internal relations became "vertical," with orders flowing from the national headquarters of the union out to the locals. National union leadership knew that it had to "hold up its end of the bargain" with corporate management, even when this meant enforcing it against the will of some rank-and-file local union members.

The implications of this quest for contractual security did not stop there. The unions sought to involve the government in ensuring the legitimacy of their contracts. This necessitated the sort of practical politics that third parties could not provide. As the CIO unions grew, they tied themselves to the New Deal coalition of the Democratic Party. This was the way to get the legislation, executive branch enforcement, and judicial rulings needed to uphold the existence of the new unions. This political bargain went beyond swearing off third party politics. It also implied the acceptance of existing legal limitations, court orders, and injunctions, until they could be overturned through political action. Thus, when the sitdown strike was outlawed, or when a judge issued an injunction, labor leaders advocated compliance rather than defiance. And, in this sort of situation, rather than turn to their rank-and-file members, they turned to their political "allies."

This emphasis on contractual security also involved recognition of management's right to manage—what has become known in modern contract language as "management prerogatives"—and a commitment not to strike for the duration of the term of the contract. Even the earliest CIO collective bargaining agreements traded the right to strike during the contract period for a grievance procedure. The typical grievance procedure ensured uninterrupted production by requiring workers to stay on the job while their grievance went through a variety of steps— the foreperson and the shop steward; then the labor relations department and the union shop chairperson; then the company's main office and a representative of the international union. Some grievance procedures added a final step in which an outside arbitrator was to issue a decision. Meanwhile, the worker kept working under management's direction, or suffered the punishment management had meted out. In short, under the grievance procedure, the worker was "guilty until proven innocent." Perhaps even more importantly, it took the resolution of disagreements off the shopfloor and out of the hands of rank-and-file workers and put them in the hands of full-time union officials.

To be sure, if grievance procedures did not bring "justice" to the shopfloor, they did provide workers with some modicum of protection from management. There is certainly no comparison between working under a contractual grievance procedure and working in an "at will" setting. But, historically, the coming of the grievance procedure undermined the use of direct action as a way of resolving disagreements. Of course, workers continued to practice direct action, and would do so for years and years, but the labor agreement now denied the legitimacy of such behavior, union officials refused to sanction it, and the government refused to protect it.

Even before World War II, the new CIO unions had taken major steps in the direction of "business unionism." The centerpiece of union leaders' strategies was the "security" provided by a contract negotiated at a national level with management and enforced by the legal system. They were already showing a willingness to sacrifice direct action, sitdown strikes, defiance of judges and legal authorities, third party politics, inter-union solidarity, and organizing the unorganized on the altar of "the contract." World War II pushed the labor movement further in this direction. It widened the gap between union leaders and their rank-and-file, and it encouraged leaders to look to corporate management and the government for their legitimacy, rather than to their own members.

The organizing core of the new CIO unions in the 1930s had been informal work groups, what labor activist Stan Weir calls "workers' families on the job." These groups had grown especially close-knit during the Great Depression. In the 1920s, many corporate employers had implemented seniority provisions, which meant that older workers were not the first let go during the hard times of the 1930s. Depression also slowed the pace of technological change, leaving the organization of production fairly stable. As a result, informal work groups in most factories, mines, and mills were built on years of familiarity and mutual dependence. These groups were often the key structures in the on-the-job actions, strikes, and unionizing campaigns that swept U.S. industry between 1935 and 1938. Futhermore, once unions came into existence, these groups provided informal mediation between the union leadership and the stewards on the one hand, and individual members on the other.

But World War II disrupted these groups. As Weir puts it, they were "confetti-ized." Many union activists, even men in their thirties and forties, so identified with the war effort (the "good war," as Studs Terkel calls it) that they volunteered to fight. Production in many factories was "converted" from consumer goods to war-time goods, from autos, refrigerators, and the like, to tanks, airplanes, and torpedoes. As these factories expanded, thousands and thousands of new workers entered. Thus, the war transformed the organization of production and shifted the make-up of the workforce. New informal work groups would be constructed, but the ones that carried the experience of the organizing drives and the responsibilities for the day-to-day functioning of the industrial unions had been tossed around like confetti.

As union leaders looked out over this new workforce, they had ample reason to worry. Most of these new workers had little experience with industrial work, let alone unions. Many were women and/or agricultural workers from the South. If corporate management had chosen to undermine the still-new unions, they probably would have succeeded.

But the government loomed as a significant interested party in this situation. It wanted cooperation with the conversion to military production and the guarantee of uninterrupted production. They stepped into the labor-management relationship in ways that went far beyond their enforcement role of the later 1930s, or even their intervention during World War I. The government offered corporate management "cost-plus" contracts to guarantee that they would profit from the conversion to military production. They then encouraged management to offer unions a closed shop. In turn, the unions would offer a "no-strike pledge" for the duration of the war. Corporate management even went one step further. They offered a "dues check-off"—to deduct union dues from workers' pay checks.

In other words, the government became the unions' primary "organizer," and corporate management became the union "treasurer." The union, in turn, began to act as a party independent of the membership, even to the extent of enforcing the no-strike pledge when "wildcats" broke out. Under these conditions, union membership swelled from nine million to fourteen million over the course of the war. But many of these members now belonged to bureaucratic organizations that gave them little role to play or little voice.

At the end of the war, workers and their unions were once again engulfed in a period of instability and turmoil. Peace meant that production in many key factories and mills would be reconverted to consumer goods, and that many soldiers would be returning to reclaim their jobs. The "confetti-ization" process continued, demobilizing the rank-and-file and further empowering the union leadership. There were also deeply felt fears that, with the end of the war and its stimulation of the economy, depression conditions might set in again. Overtime work, which had been plentiful during the war, disappeared overnight, and take-home pay packets shrunk.

In this climate, the no-longer-so-new industrial unions launched a series of massive, industry-wide strikes for substantial wage increases. They demanded these increases be granted across the board, the same percentage for all workers in the industry. They also demanded that these wage increases *not* be passed along to consumers in the form of price increases. In late 1945 and throughout 1946, strikes swept U.S. industry on a scale not seen in a decade. These strikes were not coordinated across industry (and union) lines, although some occurred simultaneously and rank-and-filers often organized support for each other.

These strikes might well have had the potential to alter the trajectory unions were on. But their consequences proved only to confirm and strengthen this trajectory. The strikes themselves were never linked by union officials. More importantly, most were settled through a simple compromise—the unions were granted the wage increases, but the corporations were allowed to raise their prices. The unions had taken a major step in turning themselves into "interest" groups, acting on behalf of their own members, but not on behalf of a larger *labor movement,* and certainly not on behalf of the working class.

A year later, the infamous Taft-Hartley Act weakened labor even further. It proscribed many traditional union activities as "unfair labor practices"—most importantly, those which expressed active solidarity. It also ensured unions the protections of the law as long as they played "by the rules"—rules that made them "interest groups" able to bargain only on behalf of their own members. The consequences were far reaching.

Taft-Hartley banned two of the most important solidarity actions in labor history—sympathy strikes and secondary boycotts. It said that unions with valid contracts could not strike in support of other unions, that the only legitimate basis for a strike was a direct disagreement with one's own employer. Unions which violated this law—and their contracts—through sympathy strike action could face legal action, damages, and heavy fines. This would become the basis for pressuring unionized workers to cross other workers' picket lines. Similarly, Taft-Hartley limited the legal acceptability of boycotts to direct conflicts between workers and their own employers. Unions could no longer seek to extend boycott action to other related companies in an effort to increase their clout or the base of involvement.

These provisions of Taft-Hartley "outlawed" the two most active expressions of solidarity and sent the message that unions would be tolerated only if they stayed within the confines of a labor relations system that recognized and protected direct bargaining relations between an employer and the union that represented its employees. Yet, it didn't stop there. Taft-Hartley also required unions to sign a "noncommunist affidavit" in order to claim even these limited legal protections. Unions had to swear that they had no "communists" in leadership positions. Otherwise, they had no legal standing in the eyes of the National Labor Relations Board or the entire system that it upheld. Some union leaders or staffers resigned and some were fired or expelled in order to satisfy this provision. The unions that refused to sign this affidavit not only lost their legal status, but the CIO soon expelled them.

This had a tremendous impact on unions' efforts to expand their organization. There were two major organizing campaigns taking place at this time—one aimed at white-collar bank employees, and another called "Operation Dixie," sought to establish a union presence in the largely non-union South. The major push in both drives came from some of these expelled unions. In the wake of Taft-Hartley, both of these vital organizing campaigns ground to a halt.

The focus of expanding union membership shifted away from bringing in people who were new to unions altogether (i.e., "organizing the unorganized"). In its place, an orgy of "raiding"—cannibalism—swept through the labor movement as existing unions, or newly created anti-communist unions, launched raids on the memberships of the ousted unions. The process was simple. A raiding union distributed cards in a workplace already organized by one of the other unions. When they got 30 percent to sign, they approached the NLRB, who would then authorize an election. Since the union already present had not signed the non-communist affidavit, the NLRB refused to list their name on the ballot. The only choices to appear would be the new union or "no union." The existing union then had to urge its members to vote for the "no union" option. If it were successful, it would then have to approach the employer and ask to maintain recognition. If the employer said no, the union then had to take its members out on strike for recognition. Considering that it had just asked these people to vote for "no union," it is easy imagine how difficult this process became for the expelled unions.

This situation encouraged membership raids on other unions. Union leaders knew that it was far easier to convince people who already belonged to a union to switch, than it was to organize, often in a hostile environment, new people who had never belonged to a union before. From this point on, most union growth came from the expansion of existing units (until the organizing of public employees in the 1960s), and no further beachheads were made in key parts of the traditional non-union sea, like the South, or banking, or white-collar work in general.

The year 1948 saw the final broad-based, progressive, third party, national, political campaign in the United States—that of Henry Wallace for president. Wallace, the former New Deal vice president, drew significant labor support. But the political climate in America was becoming increasingly hysterical about a "communist threat," and as the red-baiting of his campaign grew, support for Wallace shrivelled. Meanwhile, the Democratic Party and its allies in the union leadership strengthened their relationship. All alternatives were being relegated to an increasingly marginal radical "fringe."

The mid-1950s merger of the AFL and the CIO was an anti-climactic symbol of the labor movement's capitulation to business unionism. The range of options within the labor movement had narrowed. Two key elements of the context should not be downplayed—the strength of the Cold War and anti-communism on the one hand, and the impact of Keynesian-generated economic growth on the other. That is, while the system of labor relations was maturing and unions were adjusting to it, rank-and-file workers experienced a rising standard of living over a more prolonged period than any generation of U.S. workers had ever known. They also reasonably expected even better for their children. At the same time, they saw what severe punishment could be meted out to those who stepped outside the bounds of the system. Thus, there was little rank-and-file resistance to union co-optation.

Kim Moody, in his valuable study *An Injury to All*, has captured the nature of this adaptation:

> Business unionism as an outlook is fundamentally conservative in that it leaves unquestioned capital's dominance, both on the job and in society as a whole. Instead, it seeks only to negotiate the price of this domination. This it does through the businesslike negotiation of a contractual relationship with a limited sector of capital and for a limited portion of the working class. While this political coloration of American business unionism may range from conservative to liberal, it is the bread-and-butter tradeoff—wages and benefits defined in contractual language—that concerns the business unionist...The notion of a balance of class forces between labor and capital as a whole is foreign to the business unionist...Thus, it is difficult if not impossible for the business unionist to comprehend a shift in power

relations between social classes in any terms other than the profit margins or market shares of specific employers, votes taken by 'friends' and enemies in legislatures, or the dollars and cents of influence peddling.

It was, of course, just such a "shift in power relations between social classes" that took place in America between the mid-1960s and the mid-1970s, becoming obvious with the union disaster of the 1980s. The unions, well-schooled in this system of labor relations, were ill-prepared to deal with such a change in the overall climate.

Between 1965 and 1975, a variety of factors combined to bring the postwar period of economic expansion to a halt—the rebuilding of the Japanese and West German economies and the consequent increase in international competition; declining profit rates for most corporate enterprises; the domestic pressures of the environmental and health and safety movements; the expenses of both the Vietnam War and the Great Society programs; the energy crisis and the rise in oil prices; the emergence of "stagflation"; the "blue collar blues"; even the political instability of the Johnson, Nixon, Ford, and Carter administrations.

In this changed environment, U.S. corporations launched new strategies, strategies so different from those of the 1945-1965 period that economists like Barry Bluestone and Bennett Harrison have called them a "great u-turn." These strategies included diversification (especially shifting away from manufacturing), globalization (moving operations around the world), and increased speculation. They also included efforts to roll back the influence of the government in the day-to-day functioning of the economy and labor relations—"deregulation" and "privatization"—as well as shifts in tax policies. The Republican ascendancy of the 1980s facilitated the implementation of these strategies.

Equally important were the new strategies adopted towards labor (what Bluestone and Harrison call a "zap labor" strategy). Corporate management was no longer interested in the status quo of 1945-1965, a "social contract" that tolerated unions who stayed within the confines of the labor relations system and rewarded productivity gains with wage increases. Unions were now perceived as an unwanted impediment to corporate goals—an impediment that could fairly easily be removed.

With the support of the government and the assistance of consultants, corporate management launched its aggressive anti-labor strategy. The consequences of that offensive sketched out at the beginning of this chapter confirm Kim Moody's conclusion: "Business unionism was in no way prepared to deal with increased employer confrontation." The activists of Local P-9 sought an alternative response to the current labor crisis.

Chapter 2

P-9's Militant Predecessor

When I first walked into the Austin Labor Center in the fall of 1984 my eye was attracted to a wall display of old union buttons. At first glance they appeared to be from the Industrial Workers of the World (IWW). There was the familiar globe with the latitude and longitude lines. But upon closer examination I discovered that they read "IUAW" rather than "IWW." They were dues buttons, each a different color, denoting a different month. They ran from the summer of 1933 to the spring of 1937.

My historian's curiosity was awakened—what was this organization? I asked around. The first few people I approached could tell me little or nothing. Finally, someone said: "Why, that was the Independent Union of All Workers. They were the first union here in the Hormel plant, and they organized everyone in town." Overhearing the conversation, another person added: "They were started by old Frank Ellis. He was something else. He used to say that if you were any part of the food chain, from a producer to a consumer, you all belonged in the same union."

I was intrigued by the story of the Independent Union of All Workers. I was also intrigued by the general lack of knowledge about them among the P-9ers. Indeed, their own vision of their past seemed to hinge more on old-timers' recollections about the paternalism of the Hormel family. Upon entering Austin, you saw plenty of lawn signs stencilled, "Jay Hormel Cared" but none reading, "Remember the Independent Union of All Workers." More P-9ers talked about the 50 years of labor peace that were clearly coming to an end than about the unusual roots of their union.

As the struggle deepened though, interest in the Independent Union of All Workers grew. I began doing historical research on it, together with other P-9 supporters who shared my interest. Dave Riehle, a railroad worker and union activist from the Twin Cities; Roger Horowitz, then a graduate student in labor history at the University of Wisconsin; and I frequently found ourselves handing back the real history of the union to current-day activists. Much of what we learned came from talking with IUAW veterans who still lived in Austin or from poring over old newspapers. We were struck by the degree to which history seemed to be repeating itself.

Local P-9's attempt to meet the crisis of labor head on, and provide a needed alternative to business unionism, was clearly not without historical precedent. Digging up this history seemed valuable to me, and to a surprising number of P-9 activists, on two grounds, both of which are borne out by the experience of the Independent Union of All Workers. In the first place, we felt we might find strategies and tactics that worked well then and might work well *now*. In the second place, a careful reconstruction of the past might help us understand how the present came to assume the shape it has. The history of the IUAW provides substance in both these areas.

Between 1933 and 1937, the IUAW came out of Austin and spread to at least thirteen other communities in the upper midwest. It also influenced activists in dozens of other communities. The IUAW attempted to organize "wall-to-wall," usually starting with the largest concentration of industrial workers in town and then using their collective power—as organizers, picketers, consumers, and voters—to organize others. Their efforts—expressed in organizing drives, strikes, strike support, local politics, and various cultural activities—threatened entrenched power throughout the region.

Frank Ellis was the recognized architect of the IUAW. He was already a much travelled, seasoned labor activist by the Great Depression. His experiences spanned the 1904 meatpacking strike in St. Joseph, Missouri, the free speech fights of the IWW, and the 1921-1922 national meatpacking strike. Over three decades of activism, Ellis had been jailed numerous times, had become a skilled packinghouse worker, had served on the national executive board of the IWW, and had developed his own vision of union philosophy and structure. He was skeptical of electoral politics and downright hostile to craft unionism. He believed in union democracy, shopfloor organization, direct action, an industrial structure, and solidarity among all workers. Ellis' ideas shaped the new union while his feisty bearing and distrust of authority infused it.

But Ellis certainly did not build the IUAW all by himself. Much of the drive behind the organization came from the hog kill gang. This group of workers in charge of pig slaughtering at the Hormel plant were young, lifelong, Austin residents, many of whom had been influenced by Trotskyism. Their vision of unionism—the sort of unionism needed by U.S. workers at the depths of the Great Depression—paralleled Ellis'. Ellis and the hog kill gang also drew on the involvement of a group of Communists (who were mostly based in the beef kill in the Hormel plant), several independent socialists, and other veteran trade unionists. Through 1936, these disparate elements forged a lively coalition within the IUAW, built on their contacts with activists in other cities, and nourished the growth of this remarkable organization.

The Hormel workforce was the IUAW's initial base, and it was built solidly from the ground up. The activists knew the importance of a strong shopfloor presence. "You worked with a group of people who have never belonged to a union, who have never spoken back to a foreman, and a company that didn't want to recognize you," recalled one radical. They knew that the shopfloor itself held the key to dispelling the atmosphere of fear that had held the rank-and-file back and in demonstrating the potential power of collective action.

In the summer of 1933, the hog kill gang and Frank Ellis developed a plan. They chose a highly symbolic issue to provoke a shopfloor confrontation which they would then use to launch the union. A cornerstone of Hormel paternalism had long been the Austin Community Chest. The company sought 100 percent participation by its workers. When pledge cards were distributed, one veteran recalled, "The foreman just backed you up against the wall and told you you were going to give. If you didn't, it meant your job." Bad enough when times were good, this added insult to injury in a context of lay-offs, short weeks, and wage cuts. "This was for the poor people," recalled another old-timer. "Hell, *we* were the poor people!" Over the 4th of July holiday, Hormel announced a $1.20 a week raise—and a new pension plan to be funded by payroll deductions of $1.20 a week! Pledge cards for the pension plan were to be distributed by foremen with the pledge cards for the annual Community Chest drive.

On July 13, 1933, pledge cards were distributed to the hog kill gang. When one worker yielded to the foreman's pressure and signed, the radicals stopped work. The rest of the gang followed suit. They surrounded the foreman and insisted that he tear up the card. For ten minutes, no hogs were slaughtered. Then the foreman gave in. That afternoon, word of this action spread throughout the plant, together with news of a meeting to be held after work in Sutton Park.

The Hormel workers were electrified by the hog kill action. One later described the atmosphere surrounding the meeting:

> I saw a man walking his way toward the park. His back was bent from the toil of pulling trucks, but he walked with a purpose toward this meeting. I don't know what his thoughts were, possibly better days to come...The speaker spoke about the benefits of organization. You could see the purpose in the eyes of these fellows. I looked at their eyes. New hope was shining in them.

Ellis chaired the meeting. Several speakers—women as well as men—urged the crowd to organize. Ellis laid out his vision of an organization that would reach all workers in Austin, as well as promote the national unionization of the meatpacking industry along industrial lines. The new union was to be open to "all wage earners, no matter where employed..." Undaunted by the presence of company stool pigeons, 600 signed up.

Twice more in the ensuing months, the IUAW relied on visible workplace confrontations to build the union. Each time, they not only demonstrated their strength to the company, but also demonstrated the workers' own strength to themselves. Direct action was the IUAW's pre-eminent tactic. It was through mass direct action that they got union recognition to begin with. On September 23, 1933, while Ellis was behind closed doors bargaining with Jay Hormel, workers massed at the front gates and refused to go in. Hormel and Ellis came out and addressed the crowd from a hastily assembled platform. Ellis—the veteran soapboxer—stood his ground, as did the crowd. Hormel yielded and signed an agreement in front of everyone right at the gate.

Despite the formal recognition, the wage increase so desperately needed was not forthcoming. Once again, the IUAW turned to mass direct action. Following a tumultuous union meeting on Friday night, November 10, which heard a report of no progress in wage negotiations, the hog kill gang went directly to the plant. One of them recalled: "We rushed to the packinghouse and we took over. We told the sheep kill gang [which worked the late night shift] to clean the sheep, put them in the cooler, and get the hell out." For the next three days, in what some labor historians consider to be the first "sitdown" strike of the 1930s, the IUAW maintained control of the plant. Governor Floyd Olson, a leader of the Minnesota Farmer Labor Party, rushed to Austin, where he mediated an agreement between Jay Hormel and the union. A mass meeting at the state armory overwhelmingly approved it.

The IUAW continued to maintain a strong shopfloor presence in the Hormel plant. Each department elected a three-person committee, and each committee elected a chairperson. Although the agreement established a formal grievance procedure with arbitration, the union relied largely on direct action—slowdowns, sitdowns—to resolve grievances on the spot. One union veteran offered this description:

> Frank Ellis would sit down in the union hall. They would call him up and say: "Come on over, the department is sitting down..." So over Frank goes. Frank would go over to the hog kill or the hog cut or one of the departments, and here the people were madder than hell, sitting against the wall, refusing to work. And then the company would meet with Frank, and Frank was 175 percent for the worker...You never had to worry about Frank seeing the company side of anything. They'd get the grievance settled right on the job.

Ellis himself explained to an interviewer:

> Most of our strikes were sitdown, sitdown right on the job and not do a damn bit of work until we got it settled...We had strikes every day. Hell, if a fellow farted crooked we would strike about it.

From its base in the Hormel plant, the IUAW spread throughout Austin and into other communities. Many of the rank-and-file packinghouse workers—out of the hog kill, the beef kill, the loading dock, and the sausage department—put in long hours as volunteer union organizers. In Austin, the union reached its goal of 100 percent unionization. It included "units" of truckers and warehouse workers, barbers and beauticians, waiters, waitresses and bartenders, construction tradesmen and laborers, WPA laborers, automobile mechanics and service station attendants, laundry and dry cleaning workers, retail clerks, and municipal employees. From beauty shops with three employees to the local Montgomery Wards, every retail and service establishment in Austin came under contract with the IUAW.

The IUAW built its strength through a variety of tactics. At times, they relied on the direct action of workers in these industries. During strikes, other IUAW members provided material aid to strikers and their families. The expansion of the IUAW also rested on the collective consuming power of the Hormel workers, expressed through consumer boycotts. And, here and there, creative picketing tactics were employed. During a strike against a transfer company, for example, mobile pickets were dispatched to rural roads outside Austin to block delivery trucks. On several occasions, the IUAW actually hired unemployed workers to put in daily shifts as pickets in front of retail establishments. They showed a particular willingness to ignore court injunctions (which were handed out so frequently against IUAW actions that the local judge was nicknamed "Injunction" Peterson) and go to jail, if need be.

The IUAW also sought allies outside the boundaries of the formal labor movement. The family farmers in southern Minnesota and northern Iowa had been hard hit by the Great Depression. Both land values and prices for farm products had plummeted, but banks had demonstrated little sympathy for the farmers' plight, and had launched an aggressive campaign of mortgage foreclosures. Farmers in the region organized the Farm Holiday Association (FHA), which employed creative, militant tactics such as withholding their crops from market and interfering with foreclosure auctions. Solidarity between the IUAW and the FHA flowed in both directions. IUAW members participated in FHA picket and "penny auctions," while FHA members provided IUAW strikers with food or even joined their picket lines.

The IUAW also built a rich, active culture for its members, especially in Austin. There was the *Unionist,* delivered free on Friday mornings to every household in Austin. It was edited by Carl Nilson, a Trotskyist from the Twin Cities who had come to Austin under the auspices of the state Bureau of Workers Education. The first issue of the *Unionist,* in October 1935, declared: "In line with the history and tradition of the union, this paper will be radical and militant, dynamic rather than static, alive rather than asleep." It certainly tended to live up to its own billing. A union veteran, only a teenager in the IUAW period, recalled:

> The *Unionist* has had a terrific influence in educating our members, tempering the vociferousness of the ene-mies of organized labor, organizing the unorganized and speaking out for the oppressed and downtrodden people who otherwise could not make their voices or grievances known.

In addition to editing the *Unionist,* Nilson taught classes in public speaking, parliamentary law, labor history, economics, and current events. He also organized classes in band, chorus, and dramatics that played an important part in the culture of the IUAW. The union and its women's auxiliary organized a lively drum and bugle corps, which led many parades, and a drama troupe which performed several plays. These activities raised funds for the union, educated both participants and audience, and added to the rank-and-file's sense of unity and identity. The IUAW also established a library in the union hall, which featured works by Edward Bellamy, John Reed, and Upton Sinclair. The *Unionist* included a regular book review column, written by Nilson's wife, Marian (whose father had been a Knights of Labor activist in the 1880s).

In the summer of 1937, an IUAW activist looked back over the accomplishments of its four-year history:

> Since 1933 the workers in Austin have never let up their efforts to make Austin 100 percent union...Above all, Austin's unionization is not a shallow thing, but a master organization that penetrates far into the very lives of the workers that live in Austin...It is not merely a matter of wages and more money to spend. Within this program

of unionization lies the basis of things that are far reaching and more important. With unionization comes a new freedom—a freedom of the individual that will grow in importance as the organizational experience grows older. A new freedom of thought, of action and knowledge, are products of workers' lives protected through organizations of their own choosing.

The IUAW was structured to maximize participation in running the union. "Units" met on a weekly basis, with all rank-and-filers able to shape union policy for their industry. "Local 1," which consisted of delegates elected by each Austin unit, met monthly and considered issues of concern to the entire IUAW. Once a week there was an open mass meeting—"the big meeting," one union veteran recalled, "to have a solidarity of the masses, as Frank Ellis used to talk about." These mass meetings did not take formal votes or set specific policy for the union, but they brought together rank-and-filers and auxiliary members from across the city to hear speakers, debate political issues, and map out solidarity campaigns.

Over the next four years, the IUAW organized in more than a dozen communities outside Austin. Their outreach strategy was more of the same: organize the largest group of industrial workers in the community, then use their power to bring organization to other workers, meanwhile building a lively movement culture. They succeeded, to varying degrees, in Albert Lea, Faribault, Owatonna, Rochester, South St. Paul, Bemidji, and Thief River Falls, Minnesota; Madison and Mitchell, South Dakota; Fargo, North Dakota; Algona, Mason City, Waterloo, Cedar Rapids, Ottumwa, Fort Dodge, and Estherville, Iowa; Alma and Madison, Wisconsin. In some places, permanent IUAW "Local Unions" were established. In others, organization ebbed and flowed. The IUAW also supported union campaigns in Minneapolis, St. Paul, Omaha, Sioux Falls, Sioux City, and even Kansas City and Oklahoma City.

Typically, Austin activists connected with radicals and veteran unionists in packing plants and factories, who were frustrated with the inadequacies of AFL unionism and in search of a new approach. Austin activists led organizing teams on forays into these communities. Their initial activities involved some spirited public speaking, Ellis usually getting top billing. His approach was well thought out. He "would set a group of workers on edge for a few weeks, get them to do some thinking," recalled one old-timer. Another union veteran hailed Ellis as an "agitational speaker" who "managed to capture workers' restlessness." His blunt style seems to have been effective. "Whenever you mentioned the AFL, he'd spit on the ground," recalled another.

Ellis and other IUAW organizers would point to their success in Austin and emphasize that much the same could be accomplished in other communities. Indeed, they readily offered the support of the well-organized Austin workers. In February 1935, for example, Ellis told a mass meeting of Rath packinghouse workers about to go on strike in Waterloo, Iowa:

> If you say so, we'll bring in militant workers from other cities who will put this thing over. We'll shut down the packinghouses in Austin and Albert Lea if necessary to get men in here to win this strike.

Some IUAW organizers would usually stay in these outposts, assisting local activists with the day-to-day work of getting their organization off the ground. Some offered special expertise. Joe Voorhees, a former schoolteacher who had become Ellis' right hand man as well as a core member of the Trotskyist group, often helped lay the basis for a solid, democratic organization. Carl Nilson frequently helped with writing and publishing leaflets or even local newspapers.

Once workers began to organize, moreover, they could count on the continued support and solidarity of the well-organized Austin unionists. In July 1935, for example, the IUAW coordinated a series of sympathy strikes by more than 1,000 Wilson packinghouse workers in Albert Lea and Faribault, in support of 100 striking Wilson poultry plant workers in Faribault. In January 1935 and again in April 1937, Austin IUAWers responded en masse to an "SOS call from Albert Lea." Both times, they joined in mass street fights with squads of special deputies. Between late 1936 and early 1937, Austin activists provided similar physical support to Tobin packinghouse strikers in Fort Dodge and Estherville, Iowa.

The IUAW provided a cohesive network for labor activism in these far-flung communities. Annual conventions brought together formal delegates from each "Local Union," both to handle union business and to picnic and commune together. "Wall-to-wall," 100 percent unionism, may never have been achieved in all these communities, but a powerful foundation was laid for the development of permanent union organization. In some communities, IUAW activists entered local and regional politics, usually through "farmer-labor" formations. In Austin and Albert Lea, for instance, they captured seats on the city council and became a force in the congressional district.

The Hormel packinghouse activists who built and extended the Independent Union of All Workers wrestled with a difficult problem, however. Hormel management insisted that raises given to their workers would have to be linked to raises achieved by packinghouse workers throughout the country. This pressure helped extend the IUAW. It also led Austin activists to meet with packinghouse unionists from around the midwest to discuss linking up their activities, if not their organizations. After the CIO was formed in 1935, some of the activists contacted John L. Lewis and asked for his help. In these efforts they continued to face a dilemma: how to build a cohesive national organization that would still rest on the local democracy and horizontal solidarity that had been the lifeblood of the IUAW.

The activists who belonged to Communist and Trotskyist parties tended to short-circuit the resolution of this dilemma. Some, particularly the Communists, had little concern for local democracy *per se.* They were more concerned with other goals, such as building a larger CIO to counter-balance the AFL, and ironing out formal union policies. The Trotskyists had their own agenda, too, one that emphasized work inside the major formations within the labor movement, either AFL or CIO, rather than taking up independent positions outside these structures. Both groups, regardless of mutual hostility, promoted affiliation with the CIO at the earliest possible date.

Ellis was the strongest voice of skepticism towards this goal. However, at a critical point in the debate, he was out of the picture, locked away in the state prison on trumped up charges. Ellis did not idealize some sort of local autonomy for the IUAW. In fact, he had participated in various formations, such as the Northwest Labor Unity conferences, and meetings with packinghouse unionists from around the country. He sought, however, to maintain the network of horizontal solidarity and the practice of local democracy that had typified the

IUAW. Since the CIO did not yet have specific affiliates or organizing committees for all industries, there was also the problem of maintaining the inclusion of all the workers who had been part of the IUAW.

Suddenly in the spring of 1937, crisis forced the IUAW to settle on a course for its future. The unfolding of this crisis allowed for little consideration of the sort of issues that Ellis emphasized. And it sealed the fate of the Independent Union of All Workers. On March 8, 1937, truck drivers and warehouse workers at two transfer companies in Albert Lea (20 miles west of Austin) went on strike. Carl Nilson, who had given up the editorship of the *Unionist* to take the lead in organizing truckers in southern Minnesota and northern Iowa into the IUAW, coordinated the Albert Lea strike. In a matter of days, freight began to pile up at the railroad station. The truckers were well-organized and had been a "unit" within the IUAW for some time.

The situation in Albert Lea took on new proportions as other dramatic strikes began to break out. On March 18, a dozen young women clerks began a sitdown strike at Woolworth's. They had been in the IUAW for some time, but negotiations for formal recognition, wage increases, and seniority protections had been going nowhere. They knew that the IUAW had successfully organized the Montgomery Wards in Austin as well as smaller retail establishments. Ray Hemenway, the most militant and best known IUAW activist in Albert Lea, was handling the negotiations on their behalf. Described as "part Wobbly, part Trotskyist" by one old-timer, Hemenway sat on the IUAW executive board as well as leading "Local Union No. 2" in Albert Lea. After weeks of fruitless negotiations, with the full backing of the IUAW, Hemenway and the young clerks decided the Easter shopping season was an opportune time for them to strike.

The very next day, sitdown strikes also broke out in the two plants of the American Gas Machine Company. Next to Wilson's packinghouse, they were Albert Lea's major industrial employer. Since the IUAW had expanded into Albert Lea, labor conflict had been frequent—and often violent—at American Gas. In February 1935, a brief strike at the Potter Foundry (a subcontractor of American Gas) had escalated into a walkout at the major plant and a physical confrontation between IUAW pickets and sheriff's deputies that resulted in several injuries and arrests. Half a dozen IUAW activists were sentenced to 60 days hard labor as a result of this battle, and a bitter enmity between the union and the sheriff, Helmer Myre, was established. Over the next two years, the IUAW had won grudging recognition from American Gas, which continued to provide support for a local anti-union Citizens Alliance formation. The seasonal ups and downs of American Gas Machine's business, together with the anti-unionism of its management, kept the IUAW's foothold insecure.

On March 18, the day the clerks took control of Woolworth's, American Gas management took a provocative action. They fired four IUAW activists from the main plant. Though they claimed that a business downturn had necessitated a round of lay-offs, the IUAW saw this as an attack on the union. On March 19, they initiated a sitdown strike at the company's two plants, one on Front Street and the other on Clark Street. At the latter location, strikers took up positions in the large street-level display window, waving to passers-by and demonstrating their high spirits.

For two weeks, all three strikes held firm. Nilson published a daily strike bulletin that answered the rumors and accusations appearing in Albert Lea's anti-labor paper, the *Evening Tribune.* Austin IUAW activists visited Albert Lea regularly, bringing material and moral support to the sitdown strikers. Every evening, the IUAW Drum & Bugle Corps paraded the streets of Albert Lea, marching from the Clark Street plant (where the occupiers cheered from the display windows) to the Front Street plant. From there, they marched to Woolworth's. Each night, the women occupying the store greeted the paraders with a song. Then, the parade continued to the Wittmer and Thompson & Wulff warehouses, with a side trip by the railroad depot for a progress report on the accumulating pile of freight.

Despite the spirit and unity of the strikers and their supporters, the IUAW's enemies, organized by the Albert Lea Chamber of Commerce and its "Secret Committee of 500," planned to defeat the union. This network linked Judge Cooney, the virulently anti-union vice president of Wilson, the local American Gas Machine management, experienced opponents of the IUAW (like the owner of Burnsmoor Dairies), and enemies of organized labor from the Twin Cities, such as the Minneapolis Citizens Alliance. Their scheme revolved around a city-wide company union they had created, the Albert Lea Employees Labor Association (ALELA). Jack Blades, the most notorious sheriff's deputy in town, served as its president. Their plan was to start a back-to-work movement under the auspices of this "labor" organization, denounce the interference of the "outside agitators" of the IUAW, and eventually grant formal union recognition to the ALELA.

This plan relied on cooperation from several quarters. District Court Judge Norman "Injunction" Peterson issued the necessary injunctions to order the evacuation of the plants, the warehouses, and Woolworth's. Sheriff Helmer Myre swore in 150 special deputies, many of them farmers from rural Freeborn County, or experienced anti-union private cops from the Twin Cities. The Albert Lea *Evening Tribune* berated the strikers, their "violation" of the "rights" of private property, and published the names of those who were risking arrest by ignoring Peterson's injunctions. The paper put particular pressure on the young women in Woolworth's, publishing rumors of "immoral" goings-on among the male and female occupiers. It appealed directly to their parents to pull them out, and to the young women themselves, asking them if they intended to miss out on wearing their finery in the traditional Easter parade. Daily, the *Tribune* claimed that back-to-work sentiment was growing. Its claims were further supported by the appearance of a daily ALELA newsletter, the *Labor News,* which red-baited the leadership of the IUAW and re-echoed the theme of "outside agitators." The final piece of the strategy came from the state AFL, which, in the midst of this conflict, granted the ALELA a charter!

Nevertheless, a back-to-work movement never materialized and the pickets held firm until the IUAW and the strikers finally decided to yield to the judge's injunctions. On the morning of April 2, they vacated the plants, warehouses, and department store. They took up positions as mass pickets in each location. In retrospect, this was a tactical mistake. Sheriff Myre and his deputies attacked the pickets outside the American Gas Machine plant, dispersing them under a cloud of tear gas and a barrage of rubber hoses. The "forces of order" then laid siege to the IUAW union hall, ultimately destroying it. Sixty-two men were arrested as they fled and were herded to the county jail. Among them were some IUAW activists from Austin. Ray Hemenway and some others escaped by climbing onto the roof. The scene was a chaotic, pitched battle, reminiscent of the sacking of IWW offices in the Pacific Northwest during World War I.

Word quickly reached the Hormel plant in Austin. According to some participants in the events, at least 400 men put aside their tools and walked out. They stopped at their homes to pick up assorted weapons and then drove in a caravan to Albert Lea. There, they marched down the main street to the jail and demanded that all the prisoners be freed. When the brand new Albert Lea police cruiser pulled up, the crowd surrounded it, took the cops out, rolled it over, set it on fire, and then slid the charred remains into the lake across the street. Armed with crowbars, individuals from the crowd began to pry open the bars on the windows of the jail. Seated on top of the building, a deputy either could not figure out how to operate the World War I machine gun that Sheriff Myre had obtained or was unwilling to use it. At any rate, the crowd was clearly in command of the situation.

At this dramatic moment, Governor Elmer Benson made his way through the crowd. Another Farmer-Laborite, he had won the 1936 election after the death of popular governor Floyd Olson. Benson had arrived the previous day, eager to mediate a settlement as his predecessor had done in Austin in 1933, but so far, he had had little luck. When the crowd laid siege to the jail, Benson had left the hotel and approached the jail himself. He strode forward and demanded the keys to the jail from Sheriff Myre. He then freed all the prisoners and the crowd carried them away on their shoulders. According to local lore, several prisoners being held for non-strike-related offenses (such as drunk and disorderly conduct) were so jubilant over their liberation that they joined the IUAW on the spot.

The crowd streamed back to the Clark Street plant, eager to avenge that morning's rout. They surrounded the plant, while the deputies fled up to the fourth floor. IUAW leaders negotiated the surrender of the deputies. They were forced to put their badges and weapons in boxes outside the door, and were then verbally and physically abused by a gauntlet of strikers and supporters. The IUAW was in command, from the plant itself to the very streets of Albert Lea.

That night, Governor Benson attempted to work out a negotiated settlement. The union was to call off the strike and return to work immediately. The companies were to rehire all strikers and the four IUAW members fired at American Gas. They would also recognize the IUAW and bargain with them, but on one condition—that the IUAW affiliate with a national union within 60 days. This condition was put forward by the employers, and promoted by Benson's advisers, several of whom were close to the Communist Party and were eager to build the CIO (which is where most people thought the major pieces of the IUAW would end up). With Ellis behind bars hundreds of miles away and both the Communists and the Trotskyists in favor of CIO affiliation, the IUAW accepted Benson's terms.

The consequences for the IUAW were dreadful. A month later, the Albert Lea Employees Labor Association actually defeated the CIO affiliate in an election at American Gas Machine, largely on the votes of several hundred "workers" hired after the strike—and discharged after the election. The IUAW voted city by city over the next several months to affiliate with the CIO. Some "units" never found a home with a national union and faded away altogether. The "uptown workers" of Austin—largely retail clerks, waitresses, hotel maids, beauticians, and the like—bounced from the IUAW to the Teamsters to District 50 of the United Mine Workers, losing members each step of the way.

Nilson's truckers and warehouse units in Austin, Albert Lea, Mason City and Ottumwa, left the IUAW to join the Teamsters. The national Teamsters leadership lost no time informing Nilson that since this included a relationship with the AFL, they were to have no ongoing relationship with the units of the IUAW that had affiliated with the CIO. Nilson soon lost his job as a "business agent" for these organizations and also found himself blacklisted from his former position with the state Bureau of Workers Education.

The Hormel unit affiliated with the CIO, first directly, and then with the Packinghouse Workers Organizing Committee, when it was established. Key local leaders joined the regional or national union staff and left Austin. They did indeed help build the strong national industrial organization they felt they needed, but at the expense of the local democracy and internal life that had characterized the IUAW. By World War II, a group of "straight trade unionists" had assumed the leadership of the Hormel organization, and they laid the foundation for the business unionism that would bring the union to the brink of disaster 40 years later.

Efforts to maintain the horizontal solidarity of the IUAW fell short. In late 1937, one activist—an independent socialist and then editor of the *Unionist*—promoted the formation of an "Austin Central Labor Assembly" to maintain the ties of the IUAW. It was stillborn, undermined by the distance between communities, the contention that Austin seemed to want to dominate them, and by the sectarian squabbles of Communists and Trotskyists. A year later, an effort to link all packinghouse workers in the region in a somewhat autonomous organization was scuttled by the CIO itself and its communist regional director.

Some of the activists realized what had been lost, but there was no turning back the clock. One, a veteran packinghouse worker from Omaha who described himself as influenced by Ellis' "one big union philosophy," conveyed this sense of loss in a recent interview:

> I thought we were going into an era...where we'd tell the leaders of this industrial society how we wanted the country to run. It never came out that way...I thought we'd have a case where we'd permanently make a change so that people would have much more to say about the kind of society they lived under. I know we had the foremen off balance. Don't worry, those foremen didn't get away with too much. We had democracy in most of those plants. But I thought there was a possibility [we] would make a permanent change in that direction...

Thus, the IUAW left a contradictory legacy for P-9. On the one hand, they demonstrated how to build a lively, democratic, militant labor movement, rooted in local control, committed to horizontal solidarity. On the other hand, they had not found a way to keep this alive while building a strong national organization able to control conditions in any given industry. From World War II to the late 1970s, a business unionist approach would erase much of the living memory of the IUAW. Yet, in 1985-1986, Local P-9 would emerge from the Austin Hormel plant and build on this ambiguous but important legacy.

Part II

The Hormel Strike

Chapter 3

Revitalizing the Local Union

One of the aspects of P-9 that most attracted union activists was the extent to which rank-and-file participation characterized its struggle against the Hormel Company. Many union activists continue to seek the keys to putting the movement back into the labor movement. While the P-9 experience does not yield many easily reproducible formulas, a careful retracing of its revitalization as a local union might well generate some constructive thinking.

Two important points need to be made. First, despite its deep roots in the Independent Union of All Workers, Local P-9 had become much like any other union in the United States by the 1970s. Business agents ran the union, and they relied on the grievance machinery and arbitration rather than direct action on the shopfloor. Most members barely participated in the union. Indeed, by the 1970s, getting a quorum for a union meeting was no sure thing. Second, it was management itself, in its corporate policies and its shopfloor behavior, that proved to be the major force in the revitalization of the union. Management's introduction of new technologies, its elimination of departments, its demands for wage freezes and increased production standards, and its increased pressure in the workplace itself motivated rank-and-file workers far more than any brilliant strategies by union activists. This is not to say that the revitalization of Local P-9 was an automatic or spontaneous process. A core group of local activists worked long and hard to breathe new life into this union, to involve the membership, and to challenge the corporate management.

P-9's revitalization was the product of a new generation. In 1965, Hormel began hiring in Austin for the first time since 1952. By 1970, more than 400 had been added to the workforce. Then hiring stopped. In a workplace regulated by intricate seniority provisions, most new hires were tracked into the nightshift, especially the beef departments, rather than the generally better paying pork departments. Many were the children of longtime Hormel workers, though, unlike their fathers, many of them had attended college. Some were Vietnam veterans, and some were women.

Unlike their fathers, this new generation would not find economic security and social respect through working at Hormel. Both corporate paternalism and business unionism failed them, virtually from the day they started work. Just as it was hiring new workers, the company was moving towards a take-back campaign. And the leadership of the local union, embedded in cooperative relationships with corporate management, yielded again and again.

In the 1940s and 1950s, Hormel had been hailed as an example of "industrial democracy," where workers had used a complicated system of piece rates and bonuses to maintain control over daily production. But in the 1960s, Hormel introduced time studies and tightened work standards. The union offered no resistance. On the beef side, the union agreed to lower rates for most jobs. The 1965-1970 generation found themselves stuck on nights, in the tougher jobs, and in the poorer paying departments. As Vietnam era "stagflation" set in, their real earnings began a downward slide.

The more cooperative the union tried to be, the more the company seemed to want. And they seemed to have fewer compunctions about doing whatever they deemed necessary to get it. Despite the Hormel family's repeatedly expressed commitment to Austin, corporate management acquired facilities in a dozen cities across the country. In 1966, 1976, and 1977, they handed out lay-off notices by the hundreds before or after asking for some concession. In 1976 and again in 1981-1982, they pushed hundreds of Austin workers to transfer to other plants or take severance settlements. In 1976, they eliminated the Austin beef kill. Two years later, they threatened to close the aging plant and build a new, state-of-the-art plant, outside of Austin. The union entered into a "new plant agreement" that eliminated all incentive pay, raised productivity standards by 20 percent, froze wages for seven years, and banned all strikes for three years after the new plant opened. (Where 5,000 had once worked in the old plant, no more than 1,750 would ever work in the new one.)

By this time, the 1965-1970 generation had grown frustrated with its situation and with the local's unwillingness or inability to address it. Over a ten-year period, Jim Guyette emerged as the primary spokesperson for this generation. Born and raised in Austin, he had attended the local community college and had served in the local unit of the National Guard before hiring into the plant in 1968. Like many members of this generation, he was the son and grandson of Hormel workers. Guyette demonstrated an instinct for justice, democracy, and decentralization early on. Like the rest of his generation, he began working beef on the nightshift. From the beginning, he questioned the power wielded by the pork worker majority within the local, especially when it came to setting the rates in the beef departments. Later, Guyette openly criticized an ineffectual 21-week slowdown organized by the union. He argued that it would be better to meet each morning and pick a department out of a hat to slow down that day, rather than present the company with a predictable—if lower—output. His interest in militant tactics was a challenge to business unionism.

After he transferred to the loin cooler in the mid-1970s, his new group of coworkers became the center of rank-and-file activity on the shopfloor and in the union. Their location gave them the opportunity to have contact with virtually all the departments in the plant. In 1978, they built the opposition to the no-strike clause in the "new plant agreement." Though they fell short, they generated 502 negative votes, and spawned an opposition group within the local known as the "502 Club."

Guyette and his generation were learning about solidarity from their own experiences. A year later, the nightshift loin cooler gang went on a slowdown to protest the system of "dual gains" wage payments, a practice that paid workers with higher departmental seniority more for the same job done by their workmates. The gang argued that this divided workers. They demanded that everyone in the gang be paid the same—a challenge to the local union (which had negotiated the system and had used the practice as a way to maintain the loyalty of the older workers) as well as to the company. The entire gang—including the higher seniority workers—stuck together. They picked a Thursday, the heaviest day of the week, to begin work at a "safe work pace." Both the company and the union tried to end the slowdown, but the gang held firm. In a matter of days, they had won. Word spread throughout the plant, and, with it, respect for Guyette.

In 1979, the union's internal dynamics shifted when their international merged with the United Food and Commercial Workers (UFCW). Packinghouse workers were a small minority in this new formation, less than 100,000 out of more than a million. The UFCW launched a program of merging local unions into geographic conglomerations of hundreds of disparate workplaces and thousands of unrelated members.

In the summer of 1980, Guyette—still just the nightshift loin cooler steward—led the opposition to a UFCW proposal that the Austin local merge with the local at the Fort Dodge, Iowa, Hormel plant. The company was about to close this plant, and a merger of the locals would have allowed Fort Dodge workers to transfer to Austin and use their seniority to bump local workers. Rumors persisted that the UFCW also wanted to merge P-9 into a Twin Cities-based retail local, like it had already done with many packinghouse locals. The local leadership, still relying on its base among the high seniority generation, seemed willing to go along with this agenda. When Guyette protested at a union meeting, he was ruled out of order. But he persisted and took his protest directly to the union membership. This time, they over-ruled the chair and went on to vote down the UFCW proposal. The tide was beginning to turn within the local and Guyette figured prominently in the dynamics.

In 1981, he was elected to the executive board. This entitled him to participate in local and "chain" (company-wide) negotiations. On both levels, he argued that "further concessions should not be offered to the industry's most profitable employer." On his own, he put out a bulletin to inform rank-and-filers what the company was seeking—and how little resistance the union was offering. Though both the UFCW and the P-9 executive board recommended the membership accept Hormel's demand for a wage freeze and COLA cuts, Guyette presented a minority report opposed to all give-backs. The membership voted down the Hormel proposal and endorsed the Guyette minority report.

Conflicts spilled out beyond the plant, too. Guyette and his wife, Vicky, became involved in a local controversy over control of public utilities. The new Hormel plant, unlike the old one, was not going to have its own engine room and would no longer be able to generate the town's power. When the old plant closed, Austin would have to find a new source of electric power. Northern States Power (NSP) proposed that the residents tap into its lines and buy power from them. Hormel backed this proposal and the local utilities commission endorsed this plan. P-9's business agent, Dick Schaefer, sat on the commission— where he claimed to represent himself, not the union. He voted in favor of the NSP plan. The Guyettes rallied support for an alternative approach, one that would have created a municipally-owned and -run power plant. Jim challenged Shaefer at a union meeting, driving the wedge between them even deeper. Ultimately, the NSP proposal was approved.

When the new plant opened in the summer of 1982, the workforce underwent a sudden, massive change. Hundreds of high-seniority workers opted for retirement as the old plant closed, and hundreds more followed them after they got a taste of the work in the new plant. Production was substantially restructured and work groups were broken up. Although the new plant employed more than a thousand fewer workers than the old plant had at the time of its closing, Hormel had to hire more than a thousand new workers between 1982 and 1984.

These new hires constituted a third generation in the plant. The company carefully screened them. Though some were sons and daughters or spouses of P-9ers, and some were transfers from the closed Fort Dodge plant, most had no local connections and no union experience. Most were young. This new generation knew little of the history of P-9, from the days of the Independent Union of All Workers to the developing conflicts between the local leadership and the Guyette generation.

Whether one was a veteran packinghouse worker or a new hire, however, conditions inside the new plant were a nightmare. Technological innovations were introduced with little regard for safety or adequate training. When injury problems among the new hires mounted, some recent retirees offered to come into the plant to teach them how to work safely. The company wasn't interested. There was automated batching in the dry sausage, prepared sausage, and canned meat departments; integrated computer inventory management; flexibility in hog-skinning; automated storage and retrieval systems; forklift robots; and automatic ham deboners, together with faster power saws and knives. Chain speed was so fast that workers often stumbled into one another as they fell behind. Some were seriously cut. Knives were sharpened by machine and inexperienced new hires were never taught how to hand-sharpen their own knives. Veterans complained that the knives got duller faster. Carpal tunnel syndrome became epidemic. The ratio of supervisors to workers increased. Local management dragged their feet on grievances. Since the "new plant agreement" had eliminated incentive pay provisions, workers were unable to use slowdowns to resolve issues directly, since now there was only "standard," and to fall below that was to violate the contract.

Inside and outside the plant, the pressure mounted. In February 1983, Hormel put on a second shift. It included 60 Austin natives who had transferred to other plants in 1977. They returned, but at a significant loss of seniority. In March, Hormel threatened to close their Fremont, Nebraska plant and displace 854 workers, unless the UFCW local there agreed to reopen the contract and grant concessions. Local 22 was one of those geographic agglomerations created by the UFCW, with packinghouse workers in a tiny minority. The business agent rapidly gave Hormel what it wanted.

Turmoil was sweeping the entire meatpacking industry. In April, Wilson filed for bankruptcy and cut wages from the negotiated $10.69 to $6.50. Con-Agra bought Armour, closed thirteen plants, and then reopened them on a non-union basis at $6.00 an hour. That summer another of the "Big Four," Swift, slashed its wages. In October, Morrell, a major regional packer, got its contracts reopened and its wages cut. The UFCW offered little resistance. Despite their robust economic health, Hormel announced that they wanted cuts, too. They rested their case on a "me, too" clause in the Austin contract, a clause that had historically brought Austin workers the same raises as those granted by the big national packers.

In December 1983, the P-9ers elected Jim Guyette president. The process of revitalization was still far from complete. Barely half the members participated in the election. But an inter-generational coalition of activists had begun to emerge, a "good blend," Guyette later recalled. They put forward a two-pronged program: *union democracy* and *opposition to concessions.* Here was the answer to corporate paternalism and business unionism that had been emerging on the shopfloor since the mid-1960s.

Opposed at first by both the business agent and a majority of the executive board, Guyette sought to build his base among the rank-and-file by promoting internal democracy and participation. He particularly emphasized that the membership must be well-informed in order to participate fully. He broke all precedent by sitting in on grievance hearings (the business agent's turf) and then using in-plant bulletins to inform the membership what was happening in them. Rather than edit the *Unionist* on his own, he organized a ten-member editorial board and gave them substantial responsibility in the production of the paper. Guyette also made sure that no one was denied the right to speak at a union meeting and that union policies were developed openly and democratically.

Management's behavior and conditions in the new plant certainly helped build attendance at local meetings. When it came to the new hires, Guyette later recalled, "The company was our best organizer." The new hires were not only a majority of the local, they were also a majority of the injured and maimed. When rank-and-filers came to union meetings, they discovered that their opinions counted and that they were respected. They also found the main topic of discussion was how to resist concessions. More than anything else, it was the unfairness of Hormel's demands that united the rank-and-file. Profits were up, as was productivity. Chief Executive Officer Richard Knowlton was rewarded with a salary increase of more than $200,000 a year.

Meanwhile, workers felt that even though they had sacrificed for the company, they had received only injuries and broken promises in return. In 1978, Hormel had threatened to close the Austin plant and build a new one somewhere else, unless Local P-9 agreed to a long list of concessions. Among them was the phasing-out of the traditional piece-work standard and bonus system that had been the basis for wage payments since the days of the Independent Union of All Workers. Under the terms of the "transitional" and "new plant" agreements, bonus money earned after 1978 went into escrow accounts, until it was phased out altogether. Local P-9 members agreed (under duress) to lend hundreds of thousands of dollars from these accounts, at below market interest rates, to the company for the construction of the new plant. Management promised that earnings in the new plant would never fall below those in the old plant. They also promised that new technology would make everyone's work easier. But now they wanted to reopen the contract to extract a wage concession, and workers were being injured at a record rate.

In the spring of 1984, the Hormel union "chain" (representatives of each of the locals with members in Hormel plants—most of whom were amalgamated and geographic in structure, rather than industrial) met in Chicago, where UFCW National Packinghouse Division Director Lewie Anderson presented an aggressive stance: no locals were to consent to concessions. Yet, shortly afterwards, when Hormel asked the UFCW to reopen the Ottumwa, Iowa contract, Anderson gave his okay, and failed to inform the other chain locals of the negotiations. When Guyette got wind of what was happening, he wrote three letters of protest to UFCW President William Wynn (March 19 and 30 and April 24, 1984). But Wynn refused to intervene and stop the Ottumwa talks.

The Ottumwa workers were represented by UFCW Local 431, based in Davenport, some two hours away. They were once Local 1 of the United Packinghouse Workers of America, but the UFCW had merged them into Local 431, dominated by 8,000 retail clerks. The local's secretary-treasurer and business agent, Louis DeFrieze, ran the local with a tight fist. Membership meetings were held once a year. In the plant, there were no union officers above the level of chief steward.

The Ottumwa workers tried to resist the concessions demands. They voted overwhelmingly to refuse to even reopen the contract. Hormel then laid off 444 workers and announced that they were closing the hog kill and cut and considering closing the whole plant unless the concessions were granted. DeFrieze held another vote, but again, the rank-and-file refused to reopen the contract. Hormel laid off another 114 workers. DeFrieze held a third vote on the same offer on May 25, 1984. This time, the contract was reopened and the concessions were narrowly granted, cutting wages from $10.69 to $8.75 and eliminating all bonuses. The laid-off workers were then recalled.

Hormel had the wedge they wanted. They turned to the rest of the chain and demanded the same cuts. Lewie Anderson polled the locals: Did they want to stay in the chain? Were they willing to reopen the contract? Guyette responded for P-9: They wanted to remain in the chain but would only discuss wages if the contract were reopened. When the chain met in July, Guyette argued that in light of Hormel's record profits, they should be discussing raises rather than concessions.

But Anderson countered that the cuts were inevitable and it was futile to resist. He then asked Guyette for his guarantee that P-9 would strike with the chain—if they chose to go out—in September. But Guyette argued that he could not give such promises without a membership vote. He was concerned that P-9 was still covered by the no-strike clause of the "new plant agreement."

It was on the basis of this exchange that the UFCW, and its active supporters in and around the Communist Party, would later claim that P-9 had "broken with the chain," refused to extend solidarity to the other Hormel locals, and had embarked on a path of "enterprise unionism." In reality, P-9 had become the center of resistance to concessions within the Hormel chain. Organizing this resistance, however, when most of the other locals were dominated by business agents based in retail who enjoyed the support of the National Packinghouse Division director, was no easy matter.

In April and again in July 1984, Guyette personally urged Wynn to lead the fight against concessions. By July, discussions within P-9 had turned to the idea of bringing in Ray Rogers and his Corporate Campaign, Inc., to develop a new strategy for fending off concessions. The "corporate campaign"—as applied by Ray Rogers and his associates—meant careful investigation of the financial networks that stood behind the company, and then the mobilization of rank-and-file union members and their families and supporters to put pressure on key elements of those financial networks. The idea was that these elements would, in turn, put pressure on the company to settle with the union in order to get themselves out of the spotlight.

The corporate campaign strategy had been developed by Rogers in his work on the J.P. Stevens campaign on behalf of the Amalgamated Clothing and Textile Workers Union (ACTWU) in the late 1970s. Rogers directed a pressure campaign against several New York City-based insurance companies who held large chunks of Stevens stock. This was combined with a mass media campaign highlighting the conditions in Stevens' plants in the South, as well as a nationwide boycott movement. These efforts proved successful, as Stevens eventually came to the bargaining table and negotiated with ACTWU.

In August 1984, P-9's membership rejected Hormel's demands for concessions by a vote of 92 percent to 8 percent. This led the way to a chainwide rejection of the concession demands. Hormel backed off, but announced it would wait and see what happened in the industry. Yet, by late in the summer of 1984, the die was cast. Hormel, enjoying its greatest profits ever, decided to demand another round of concessions, a round which would go beyond wages to do structural damage to the patterns of wages, benefits, and work standards in all eight of their unionized plants. The UFCW was prepared to accept and even facilitate these changes, as long as their own existence (and dues base) was protected.

In early September, Anderson convened a chain meeting in Omaha. This time, he didn't invite Guyette. Instead, he invited P-9's business agent, Dick Schaefer, perhaps the key opponent to the new direction in which the Austin local was moving. In an action that highlights the contrast between business unionism and the democratic rank-and-file unionism being developed within P-9, these "representatives" agreed to the very concessions which had just been rejected by a democratic vote of their memberships. They informed Hormel that they were willing to take cuts to $9.00. They also agreed to expiration dates which would take the five locals represented out of sync with Austin and Ottumwa.

Hormel then turned to arbitration to achieve the wage cuts it wanted in Austin. When Oscar Mayer cut its wages to $8.25 in early October, Hormel cited its "me, too" rights and got an arbitrator's okay to slash its wages to the same level—a 23 percent reduction. P-9ers were furious to discover that the arbitrator's ruling was based on wording which was not contained in the 1982 contract summary that Lewie Anderson had provided them. Hormel also got a surprise bonus from the arbitrator, who ruled that many of the new hires had been overpaid medical benefits—which they would have to repay to the company. This resulted in such huge deductions from many paychecks that some full-time workers became eligible for food stamps.

It was at this point that P-9's revitalization took another critical step—the organization of the United Support Group. In September 1984, a group of P-9ers' wives began meeting in Todd Park. They made signs and stood at the plant gates once a week for all three shifts. They wanted "to show our husbands we were behind them," one activist explained to me—only to be interrupted by another member who pointed out that "we weren't behind them, we were *beside* them." By early October, 400 women were showing up for the meetings in the park. Most were married to members of the 1965-1970 generation in the plant. (Not one husband of this first group would later cross the picket lines!) Though few knew each other, they were united in their anger at the company's behavior. A prime sparkplug in the group was Vicky Guyette.

Meeting in the park soon became awkward. With no sound system, it was hard for the hundreds of women present to hear. It was also getting cold. So they asked to meet in the Austin Labor Center. Their request was granted. Their use of the center quickly went beyond one meeting a week. They launched a food shelf in the basement, in order to help those P-9ers—disproportionally the new hires—and their families who were hit hard by the wage cut and the benefit pay-back. This food shelf became an important bridge between the second and third generations. And the more the Labor Center was used, the more the first generation—including retirees—was drawn in. The musty dungeon of a basement was transformed into a lively, thriving social center, with the food shelf, hot coffee, sandwiches, hot soup, a popcorn machine, and later, a clothing exchange, and, at Christmas time, a Santa's Workshop. The United Support Group transformed the Austin Labor Center—once the location of a local union that could not draw a quorum to its monthly meetings—into a beehive of activity. In so doing, they transformed Local P-9 from a trade union into a social movement.

From this point on, Local P-9 generated a "movement culture" much like the one built in the mid-1930s by the IUAW. Conflict with the Hormel Company and participation in the union were no longer disparate activities for the wage-earners in the house. Union activity had become a way of life for hundreds of families. This new-found social-political network became a source of education and per-sonal/collective change for them; it opened up new experiences, exposed them to new ideas, and helped build new bonds. The working people who created this "movement culture" were also changed by it. The Hormel conflict was going well beyond the normal parameters of a "labor" conflict.

Interest in Ray Rogers' corporate campaign strategy was increas-ing. On October 14, 1984, following a spirited parade, 3,000 people packed the Austin High School auditorium to hear Rogers lay out a potential campaign against Hormel. At one point, the auditorium was thrown into darkness and the strains of "We're Not Gonna Take It" reverberated throughout the room. The audience stomped and clapped in time with the beat. The spirit and the enthusiasm, the presence of spouses and children, the creativity expressed in homemade signs, masks, and pig snouts, all were indications that something special was brewing in Austin.

"We are going to collectively organize your knowledge, skills, imagination, and energies, and transform your union into a powerful political and economic force," Rogers told the crowd. His proposal rested on an analysis of the opponent and maximum mobilization of the rank-and-file, their families, friends, and the rest of the labor movement. His analysis zeroed in on First Bank Systems (FBS), the largest outside holder of Hormel stock, as well as the corporation's banker since 1927. FBS was a significant financial force in several other midwestern meatpackers, whose recent wage cuts had been cited by Hormel as justification for their demands. Rogers called for a pressure campaign directed at both Hormel and First Bank. His goal was to force the company to restore the wage and benefit cuts, without having to resort to a strike.

"P-9 Proud" became the watchword of the movement. Blue hats, T-shirts, and buttons proliferated. Rank-and-file participation was organized through a series of committees. One, for instance, was the "tool box," where rank-and-filers and support group members who had been through AA or some form of peer counseling worked in teams to help workers and their families deal with the stresses generated by the wage cuts and the benefit payback. Communication with other Hormel locals was made a top priority: rank-and-file to rank-and-file. A communications committee took shape. Soon, it was reaching out to other unions, church and community groups across the midwest. Ironically, much of this activity followed in the path blazed by the spread of the Independent Union of All Workers in the 1930s. Virtually every night of the week there was some meeting, dance, or activity at the Labor Center. Meanwhile, Rogers and his associates researched Hormel and FBS and laid plans for putting pressure on them.

The UFCW opposed these moves from the very start. William Wynn warned Rogers, in a July 1984 mailgram, that it would be "regrettable" if P-9 launched a campaign without Lewie Anderson's approval. On November 1, representatives of the UFCW, on Hormel property in Austin, distributed a letter purportedly written by the presidents of other locals in the Hormel "chain," condemning P-9 for having "withdrawn from the chain." (Remember, these local officers were far from the direct representatives of packinghouse workers. They were the untouchable bureaucratic officials who sat on top of fiefdoms composed of hundreds of little units.) Hormel itself reprinted the letter in its in-house newsletter. The UFCW also furnished a copy to the media and Lewie Anderson gave interviews in which he questioned P-9's chosen course of action.

A month later, Anderson and the National Packinghouse Committee (local officers hand-picked by Anderson) gave Rogers fifteen minutes at a Chicago meeting to lay out his program. They then informed the media that they did *not* endorse the campaign against Hormel, calling it "the wrong target at the wrong time." Instead, they called for a nationwide campaign against Con-Agra/Armour. They just happened to have on hand the pre-printed signs and posters for this campaign. The rank-and-file of the Hormel "chain" were never given a chance to vote their preference. And no campaign against Con-Agra/Armour ever got off the ground.

The P-9ers went ahead with their plans—to fight Hormel's concessions demands through a "corporate campaign" organized by Ray Rogers; to build an organized democratic movement based on the rank-and-file and their families; and to expand communications with other Hormel locals. In January 1985, a local election gave the rank-and-file an opportunity to express their views. They spoke clearly.

Dick Schaefer, the longtime business agent and opponent of Guyette's, retired. Pete Winkels, whose uncle and father were popular symbols of the turbulent IUAW years, defeated John Morrison for the post. Winkels, who often played the role of homespun philosopher, was committed to the campaign and had been outspoken in his opposition to concessions for years. Morrison, in contrast, was a leader of the dissident minority faction that opposed the campaign. They were derisively called the "P-10ers" by other P-9 activists. (Interestingly, Morrison would be among the first to cross the picket lines in February 1986. He received his reward in the summer of 1987 when he became secretary-treasurer of the post-trusteeship "Local 9.") Lynn Huston, perhaps the most active of all the new hires, was elected vice-president when another "P-10er," John Anker, stepped down. (Anker would also scab in February 1986 and then become president of the new "Local 9.") Huston, with long hair, a beard, and an earring, presented an interesting contrast to Guyette, who appeared more conservative. The old leadership was routed by the insurgent majority.

In January 1985, in the absence of support from the UFCW international, the rank-and-file voted 691-217 to assess themselves $3 per week to hire Corporate Campaign, Inc. Soon, hundreds of workers, family members, and supporters were regularly picketing Hormel's plants and offices, and First Bank's headquarters in the Twin Cities and various branches throughout the region, as well as attending and speaking up at the annual stockholders' meeting. It looked, at first, like the success of the J.P. Stevens' campaign might be repeated. The corporate campaign strategy got thrown a curveball, however, when the National Labor Relations Board upheld Hormel and First Bank's contention that this campaign was an "illegal secondary boycott" under the terms of the 1947 Taft-Hartley Act. The NLRB decision was confirmed by federal judge Edward Devitt of the U.S. Eighth Circuit, and the corporate campaign was derailed.

Local P-9 was thus faced with the choice of backing down and accepting concessions or going out on strike. For most of the union's active members and their families, there was no question which choice to make. They felt deeply wronged by Hormel, wronged beyond any specific issues that could be negotiated, bargained over, compromised on, and settled. They—and, in many cases, their parents and grandparents—had worked to make Hormel a successful company. They had worked hard, dangerous jobs for decades. They had made extra sacrifices in order to get the new plant built in Austin. But now, even though it was enjoying record profits, even though it had made promises to its workers, Hormel was asking them to accept deeper pay cuts. This time was different too because the workers had become increasingly empowered through their participation in the movement culture which had developed within and around Local P-9. They had already begun to stand up to Hormel, the bank, and even their international union. Going on strike—something which had not happened in Austin for 52 years—seemed to be merely the next logical step.

The issue was not just wages, however. The new plant had become a nightmare of injuries, especially for the new hires. Hormel management did all it could to keep the lid on this issue. Since it was self-insured, the company provided little data for scrutiny by the state department of labor or the media. Through the Hormel Foundation, corporate executives maintained a close relationship with St. Olaf, the only hospital in Austin. Hospital administrators, not surprisingly, instructed their staff not to release information on Hormel plant injuries to the media. Hormel plant management resisted Local P-9's requests to allow retirees into the plant to instruct new hires on safe work practices. They rejected the union's contract proposal to have an outside expert conduct an ergonomics study with binding recommendations. Hormel was also a loud voice in state politics, agitating for reductions in workers' compensation benefits.

In discussing their reasons for voting down the company's offer and authorizing the strike by a 93 percent margin, several rank-and-filers cited an incident in the ham-boning department in the summer of 1985. Needles to say, the pace in this department was already significantly faster than it had been in the old plant, and problems with poorly sharpened knives were widespread. There was a woman in this department who was seven month's pregnant, and she was having trouble keeping up with the pace. Several fellow workers approached the foreman, offering to trade off their less demanding jobs with her for part of each shift. The foreman refused. Shortly afterwards, the woman slipped and cut off her index finger. When P-9 representatives brought up this incident up at a bargaining session, a corporate executive said that she had probably cut her finger off intentionally in order to take advantage of Minnesota's liberal workers' compensation benefits!

To the P-9ers, Hormel's entire behavior represented a broken promise and a lack of respect. How could you compromise on basic dignity and respect? In some ways, it is hard to describe the strike vote as a "choice." It was just the right thing to do; it was an act of self-respect and basic self-defense for the Local. The decision to strike was not just motivated by gut-level opposition to the company, however. It was also grounded in a strategic evaluation of the situation.

The Local felt they were in a good position to win the strike. They expected that the company would be hurt by the withdrawal of their labor, and that, even with the problems that had arisen about targeting First Bank Systems, the corporate campaign would put financial pressure on the company. Their spirits were also boosted by the tremendous support they were receiving from labor activists in other

Hormel plants, elsewhere in the meatpacking industry, and in the Twin Cities. Even the UFCW, long suspicious of the revitalization of the Austin local, officially sanctioned the strike.

In interesting ways, P-9's revitalization had renewed its relationship to its own past, in the Independent Union of All Workers. A reliance on rank-and-file democracy, militant opposition to corporate demands, and an eagerness to extend solidarity had enabled P-9 to break through the lethargy of decades of business unionism. P-9ers followed paths to other cities that had been blazed by their grandparents. Ironically, most of them knew little of this history. But their communications teams, their nightly mass meetings, their search for creative tactics, their coalitions with farmers and other groups of workers, the involvement of their families—all harkened back to a half-century earlier. But the timeliness of these activities was unmistakable as it fired the imaginations and gained the support of hundreds of thousands of workers around the country.

Chapter 4

Solidarity and Struggle

Strike support in the 1980s was episodic and barely organized. Typically, there would be a strike, and then some activists would rush to join the picket line. They might go home beforehand to gather their friends and bring them along, and if a strike lasted a period of time, there might be some efforts at fundraising or even organizing a support demonstration. Limited as this was, these activities already went beyond the typical strike scene of the 1960s-1970s, where a few picketers leaned listlessly on their pre-printed, generic "on strike" signs.

As the corporate attack on the labor movement deepened in the 1980s, strike support activity began to get more organized. Some observers of the labor scene began to use terms like "solidarity consciousness" and "horizontal unionism" to describe this new wave of local activism. Activists in cities around the country began setting up ongoing strike support committees. While the AFL-CIO officialdom and the leadership of the international unions kept their distance from these types of activities, rank-and-file strikers and labor activists fraternized on the picket line, got to know one another, swapped stories, and formed new relationships of solidarity.

No other labor conflict in the 1980s generated more organized solidarity than the Local P-9 struggle against the Hormel Company. Indeed, rallies, parades, dances, picnics, food caravans, Christmas parties, picketing, and plant gate demonstrations attracted the greatest outpouring of labor solidarity since the 1930s. At the beginning of the strike, a P-9 artist painted a map of the United States using a dot and a line to Austin to show the sources of solidarity. By the end of the strike, the map was so filled it was impossible to pick out lines or dots. More than 3,000 local unions sent material assistance. Tens of thousands of rank-and-filers and local union officers visited Austin and offered help of one kind or another.

This strong spirit of solidarity first started at home in Austin, Minnesota. No solidarity group played a more important role than the Austin United Support Group. After the strike began, the United Support Group expanded its membership and its activities. Though the leadership remained firmly in women's hands, male retirees and husbands of women workers soon joined in. An organization of high schoolers linked to the Support Group—"P-9: The Future Generation"—was also launched. In a variety of critical activities—picketing, public speaking, peer counseling, the soup kitchen, the clothing exchange, Santa's Workshop, answering mail, sending out flyers, T-shirts, buttons, hats, tapes, etc.—distinctions between P-9 members and support group activists faded. While there continued to be formal rank-and-file meetings at which only P-9 members could vote, nightly mass meetings (often for educational and inspirational purposes) grouped union members and supporters together. Weekly pot luck suppers were another source of cohesion. "The union that eats together, stays together," became a motto of the support group.

Local P-9 also actively sought support from the rest of the country. Ray Rogers and Corporate Campaign, Inc. urged P-9 to aggressively pursue solidarity both within and outside the labor movement well before the strike began, and they developed strategies and tactics to do so successfully. As mentioned in the last chapter, the communications committee organized speaking engagements and encouraged rank-and-filers to become public speakers. Their approach was rather simple: send hundreds of rank-and-filers on the road to speak to local unions, peace groups, church groups, civil rights organizations, etc. There were also large group caravans—with motorcycles and school buses—to other Hormel plants. P-9ers leafletted at plant gates and invited other Hormel workers to their campsites for extended discussions. There were also small teams on tour, often away from home for weeks at a time.

Corporate Campaign, Inc., also helped P-9 build structures to facilitate expressions of solidarity. Three months after the strike began, they launched an "Adopt-A-Family" program which had organizational as well as material goals. Local unions were matched with a specific P-9 family, and they would pledge a fixed amount of money per month for several months. The striker's family would send photographs and information to the sponsoring local, personalizing the struggle, bonding them all together, and providing the sort of support that UFCW strike benefits of $45 a week just wouldn't cover. Not only were homes and cars saved by this program, but many long distance friendships also developed.

In addition to the travelling speakers and the "Adopt-A-Family" program, widely publicized rallies, both in Austin and elsewhere (the Twin Cities, Detroit, Boston, New York, Denver, San Francisco) contributed to the process of building solidarity. Union activists, frequently engaged in ongoing battles of their own, marched and expressed their solidarity with P-9, often drawing parallels between their own situation and the Hormel conflict. Stewards at IUE Local 201 explained in a leaflet they distributed on February 7, 1986, at their own GE plant gates in Lynn, Massachusetts:

> Working men and women in Minnesota have scratched a line in the cold hard ground and declared that they will give up no more of their pride, wages, or benefits...Their victory will be hailed as the turning point against concessions bargaining, or their loss will be another crushed union. What stands between their victory or loss is the resolve of all of us.

Shipbuilders in Pittsburgh, Maine, Los Angeles, and Alabama; steelworkers in Pittsburgh and Gary; autoworkers in St. Paul and Van Nuys; meatpackers in Chicago, Boston, Detroit, Nebraska, and Iowa all came to the conclusion that concessions could only be defeated through labor solidarity.

Support for the Hormel strike reached well beyond the labor movement, however. When this little local union, characterized by rank-and-file participation, honest leadership, internal democracy, and creative resistance to concessions, reached out for solidarity, the floodgates opened. Farmers, peace and justice activists, poor people's organizations, even environmental groups, got involved. Many activists from a variety of movements were able to see themselves in this conflict: both their anger and frustration with the "powers-that-be" and their hopes that ordinary people can indeed fight back and win.

The Twin Cities P-9 Support Committee provides a good picture of this national support effort. In the fall of 1984, Twin Cities labor solidarity activists made several visits to Austin, for parades, rallies, and informal discussions. We were very impressed. We didn't see a bunch of grim-faced men carrying pre-printed signs. Rather, we saw whole families, men, women, and children carrying hand-lettered and creatively drawn signs, each expressing intensely felt, personal as well as collective emotions. We also met trade unionists from other cities, meatpackers from Iowa and Nebraska, who had come to Austin, looking for the same spark we were looking for. Together, we felt we had found it.

On a Sunday afternoon in early March 1985, Rogers and Guyette spoke to 50 or so strike support activists at the UAW hall in St. Paul. They urged us to form an official support committee. The idea was attractive and it made our legitimacy clear. We initially modelled ourselves after the "Committee of 100" which had played such a key role in the Minneapolis Teamsters' strikes of 1934. Bud Schulte, a veteran kill floor worker and a picket captain in the recently concluded South St. Paul strike, was elected chair. Our ranks already included autoworkers, steelworkers, railworkers, meatpackers, printers, hotel and restaurant workers, and a college professor. The Twin Cities group distributed a letter to other local unionists urging support for P-9, and, over the next months, participated in demonstrations and leafletting at First Bank branches and the First Bank annual stockholders' meeting.

In the middle of the summer of 1985, as a strike loomed more and more likely, we reorganized our committee. We set up a communications center at IBEW Local 110's hall, and we began holding open weekly meetings at UAW Local 879's hall. I was elected chair and given the responsibility of holding together a rapidly expanding and increasingly diverse group. Our ranks swelled beyond trade unionists, to include leftists of several varieties, peace and justice activists, retired unionists, college students, feminists, and assorted other sympathizers. While we operated with formal agendas and votes, we tried to reach consensus on key issues and plans, since full group agreement fostered more participation and a sense of ownership among the support committee members.

When the strike began, we turned our attention to providing material assistance, particularly food. Some of the old-timers in our ranks recalled the Wilson strike of 1959 (in Albert Lea, Minnesota) and the central role that food caravans had played in supporting that struggle. We were also inclined toward collecting food because our support committee was blessed with a priceless asset—Jake Cooper. A veteran of the 1934 Teamsters' strike and the 1948 packinghouse strike, Jake had long ago taken over a family grocery store after his blacklisting from the Minnesota industrial scene. His experience, his drive, his connections with suppliers, even his own beat-up tractor-trailer (later immortalized in a mural in the Austin Labor Center), made our food caravans a huge success. They were a success not only in the amount of food delivered (hundreds of tons, often just before holidays), but also in the publicity generated for P-9. Our support, expressed in long lines of cars and in thousands of bags of groceries, let P-9ers know that they were not isolated. These caravans also served as a model for other food caravans, not only to Austin but later to striking coal miners in Appalachia.

The Twin Cities support group also helped in the civil disobedience campaign that P-9 launched to put additional pressure on Hormel after the company announced that it intended to reopen the Austin plant with scab labor on January 20, 1986—Martin Luther King Day. Nonviolent civil disobedience to keep the plant closed seemed a natural way to honor King's memory. On January 19, 1986, nearly 1,000 supporters jammed the UAW hall in St. Paul, in response to a call signed by 40 local union officers from the Twin Cities. The atmosphere was electric, from the greeting given Jim Guyette and such honored guests as Fred Dube, of the African National Congress, to the singing of "Solidarity Forever." Some 450 men and women registered that night for a "Labor Solidarity Brigade," pledging picket line support to P-9 on the very next day.

The breadth of support for this action is suggested by the list of unions and other organizations these individuals hailed from: aerospace machinists; sheet metal workers; letter carriers and postal workers; flight attendants; graphic communications workers; autoworkers; ladies' garment workers; hotel and restaurant workers; millwrights; office and professional employees; firefighters; teachers; communications workers; carpenters; teamsters; food and commercial workers (both meatpackers and clerks); public employees (AFSCME and Minnesota Association of Professional Employees); paperworkers; railway and airline clerks; oil, chemical & atomic workers; clothing and textile

workers; steelworkers; pipefitters; electricians; united electrical work-
ers; plus COACT (a low-income neighborhood action group);
Groundswell (statewide farmers' organization); Coalition of Labor
Union Women; Minnesota Public Interest Research Group; National
Lawyers Guild; Women Against Military Madness; and the University
of Minnesota Progressive Students Organization.

Early the following day, hundreds of Twin Cities activists made
good on their pledges. They joined P-9ers in a massive car blockade
and picket around the plant. A UAW activist started it by stalling his
car in front of the main gate. A gridlock soon resulted. By 9:00 A.M.,
the company announced it would not try to start production that day.
Elated, some of the crowd went to the corporate offices, and put a
padlock, provided by a rail unionist from Minneapolis, on the gates of
the company's expensive new fence. The padlock was not discovered
until lunchtime, and the management and white collar employees were
unable to get out of the facilities for lunch. The atmosphere got even
more festive and people began to sing labor songs. Folksinger Larry
Long later commemorated these events in a verse lampooning the
media: "They came looking for violence, but they got a song."

Twin Cities activists brought special expertise to the escalating
nonviolent direct action struggle. In February 1986, members of
Women Against Military Madness (WAMM), seasoned peace activists,
came to Austin and conducted workshops in civil disobedience. One
burly meatpacker later said: "When I learned what these women had
done, and that they had been arrested and survived, I realized that I
could do it, too." Later, P-9ers, the United Support Group, WAMM
members, and other Twin Cities supporters conducted a mass sit-in at
the gates to the corporate headquarters.

This was a powerful experience for the participants, especially
those who thought only "bad people" ended up in jail. Hundreds were
arrested and taken off to a variety of lock-ups; many were offered only
Hormel chili to eat. Carmine Rogers, the wife of a P-9 retiree, later
hand-painted "jailbird" badges (each of a different bird) for everyone
arrested. She explained that after she got out of jail, she went home
"feeling dirtier than I had ever felt" and scrubbed herself in the bathtub.
She realized that she wanted to provide something for people to feel
pride rather than shame about what they had done. Hence the "jailbird"
badges. When I asked her for one for my growing collection of strike

memorabilia, she said simply: "You know what you have to do to get one, professor."

The next month, Larry Long and a diverse group of Twin Cities musicians (a "New Song" duo; a feminist quartet; several folksingers; even a P-9er, Larry Schmidt, who had been arrested at the WAMM demonstration) organized a gala "Boycott Hormel" concert at the UAW hall. They released a locally produced cassette tape with the same message. Several of the songs had been written collectively with P-9ers on the picket line in Austin. The involvement of the musicians attracted the mass media and a lively audience of nearly 1,000. New "Boycott Hormel" T-shirts were sold by the support committee. That very night, 900 P-9ers met in Austin and voted overwhelmingly to continue their strike. Our concert let them know that they would not be alone.

It was in response to this shift in power in Austin, a shift in which hundreds of Twin Cities supporters had participated, that Governor Rudy Perpich sent in the National Guard. As the guard and the state police put Austin under virtual martial law, the scabs were escorted safely into the plant. Yet, there were even more impressive acts of solidarity to come. When Hormel finally reopened its Austin plant, P-9 sent roving pickets to the other Hormel plants. In Fremont, Nebraska, enough workers refused to cross the picket lines that production was disrupted for the day. Fifty were later fired. In Ottumwa, Iowa, 505 production and clerical workers respected the lines and shut down production altogether. Municipal workers refused to cross the lines to thaw out the plant's frozen sewer pipes. Hormel fired more than 500 of the Ottumwa workers and later closed the plant completely.

The Ottumwa workers' resistance and the imposition of martial law in Austin angered activists the country over. In the Twin Cities, the support committee coordinated a noisy rally of more than 500 outside the governor's residence in sub-zero temperatures and later staged a sit-in at the governor's office that lasted more than a week. College students, peace and justice activists, and P-9 retirees—folks who could afford to take a few days out of their lives—took the lead. Some clearly had done this sort of thing before. During the day, the participants in the sit-in lobbied state representatives and senators to withdraw the National Guard and repeal the 1917 "criminal syndicalism" statute which had been used against Ray Rogers. At night, they curled up in sleeping bags on the hard floor.

In early April, Local P-9 and its supporters launched another major attempt to shut the plant with mass pickets and obstruction. Six thousand labor activists from across the country flocked to Austin for a rally, and several hundred arrived a few days early, eager to express their support on the picket lines themselves. An impromptu "rally" at the plant gates on April 11 was greeted with tear gas, police violence, and arrests with serious felony charges. "Inciting to riot" warrants were issued for Rogers and Guyette. The next day, thousands marched in protest. A day later, Jesse Jackson flew into Austin, prayed with the prisoners in jail, and proclaimed: "What Selma, Alabama, was to the struggle for civil rights in the 1960s, Austin, Minnesota, is to the struggle for economic rights in the 1980s."

After this effort, supporters shifted their focus from picket line participation and material aid to defending the activists facing felony charges and promoting the boycott of Hormel products. Both projects were pursued in ways that continued to expand P-9's support—both inside and outside the labor movement. The Twin Cities P-9 Support Committee organized a legal defense committee, which secured experienced activist attorney Ken Tilsen (a key defense lawyer in the 1973 AIM/Wounded Knee cases), and sent out a public appeal with the signatures of Meridel LeSueur, Tillie Olsen, Studs Terkel, and William Kunstler, among others. Thousands of people from all over the country responded with small donations and words of encouragement drawn from their experiences with their unions, their community groups, the Grey Panthers, Mothers Against Drunk Drivers, SANE, etc. Eventually, all the felony charges (there were eighteen defendants, including Rogers and Guyette) were dropped.

While the promotion of the boycott led to predictable actions such as leafletting supermarkets, there were also other more creative strategies. For instance, in spring 1986, the P-9ers called for a "National Boycott Day." The day they picked, however, was Minnesota's fishing season opener. Our support committee was stymied. We felt a responsibility to set the pace for the rest of the country, but fishing opener in Minnesota is as holy a holiday as Christmas is to Lutherans. We relied on the experience of the fishermen and women in our committee, however, and settled on the following plan: We would station picketers (in "Boycott Hormel" and "Cram Your Spam" T-shirts) and leafletters at bottlenecks in the two highways leading to the "lake country" north of the Twin Cities. Our leaflets proclaimed, "Eat Fish and Boycott Hormel" and announced a raffle. To enter, one had to fill out a coupon and attach a non-Hormel, union-made meat product. The prize: A boat motor. We reached thousands of people, got hundreds of entries, and enjoyed ourselves in the process. Some of us distributed the same leaflets the next weekend at the Twins' home games in the Metrodome.

Over the next two years, P-9ers and their supporters tried to keep pressure on the company via the boycott. Billboards urging "Boycott Hormel for Fairness and Justice" were leased by support committees in several cities. Several committees organized benefit concerts and rallies. In November 1986, the Twin Cities P-9 Support Committee organized one of its largest events—a concert featuring Holly Near, Arlo Guthrie, John McCutcheon, and Larry Long, which filled Minneapolis' large Orchestra Hall auditorium. In the lobby, a photo display traced the role of the National Guard in breaking meatpackers' strikes in Minnesota since 1921. The audience was a mix of activists from all sorts of movements, as well as labor veterans. I overheard someone say, while waiting in line, "If the cops sealed the doors, there'd be no demonstrations of any kind in the Twin Cities for years!"

Such support clearly had a transformative impact on the P-9ers themselves. They came to see themselves in global terms, as part of a world divided between rich and poor, powerful and powerless. This development was particularly stunning given that Austin is a small, relatively conservative, virtually all-white town, over 100 miles south of the more "liberal" urban center of the Twin Cities.

Solidarity thus came to mean more than a one-way flow into Austin. The P-9ers were as quick to extend their help to someone else as they were to ask for support. Only weeks after their own strike had begun, a busload of P-9ers joined the International Association of Machinists Local 459 picket line at the Union Brass Foundry in St. Paul. They joined in parades and demonstrations—from the annual Mothers' Day March for Peace and Justice to the feminist "Women Take Back the Night" march in Minneapolis. After supportive Hormel workers in Ottumwa were fired in early 1986, P-9ers shared their food shelf and other resources with them. They even pledged—through a democratic vote at a rank-and-file meeting—not to accept a return to work themselves until every worker fired for supporting them had been returned to work as well. P-9ers were also active in the campaign to free Amon Msane, a South African union militant detained without formal charges after a tour of the United States. Similarly, they worked to free jailed American Indian Movement leader Leonard Peltier. Wherever there was a social struggle, P-9ers were present.

The rank-and-file labor solidarity movement was also transformed in the course of the Hormel strike campaign. It increasingly came into conflict with the UFCW and the national leadership of the AFL-CIO, which felt the strike movement was getting "out of hand" and threatening the future of their brand of "pure and simple" business unionism. This caused a widespread questioning of the AFL-CIO leadership, prompted greater rank-and-file independence, and spurred on efforts to push the labor movement in a more positive direction. P-9 and its supporters often devised end-runs around the labor bureaucracy's contrived obstacles, and occasionally, even launched a frontal assault on the citadels of power in their own unions.

In September 1985, for example, the Minnesota State Federation of Labor held its annual convention in St. Paul. P-9's strike against Hormel was about one month old and still enjoyed the official sanction of the UFCW (although everyone knew their leadership opposed the strike). On the eve of the convention, P-9ers and their supporters were eager to win the official blessings of the state labor federation, as this would facilitate the provision of material assistance, and it would give their morale a boost on the heels of the NLRB decision against their corporate campaign directed at the First Bank System and the federal injunction that enforced it. Minnesota State Federation President Dan Gustafson seemed to dash these hopes when he ordered the shutdown of P-9's information table the day before the convention formally opened, using the excuse that the P-9 literature included reference to First Bank and was thus illegal. Privately, he bluntly told the P-9ers at the literature table: "Your own international doesn't back you. We don't back you, and you're going to lose!"

That evening, 40 local delegates who had some affiliation with the Twin Cities P-9 Support Committee convened a gathering at the convention hotel. They were joined by a number of P-9ers. They also attracted several dozen delegates from elsewhere in Minnesota. Together, they discussed the importance of formal support for the strike and how to challenge the state labor federation on this point.

The next morning, more than 100 P-9ers formed a gauntlet outside the doors to the convention hotel. There, on the public sidewalk, they distributed their literature to the entering delegates. Many of the delegates staying at the hotel came outside in order to get the literature. When most of the delegates were seated for the official opening, the P-9 delegation made a dramatic entrance. The assemblage rose in a standing ovation.

While State Federation President Gustafson never did allow Jim Guyette to address the convention, or allow a specific resolution endorsing P-9's struggle to reach the floor, he did finally yield to a compromise motion from the floor calling for "support for all strikes going on in the state of Minnesota." Though not a complete victory, it did give the P-9ers and their supporters enough momentum to continue building support. It was not lost on any of the participants that this effort took grassroots organizing against the state AFL-CIO leadership.

Nor was it lost on the P-9 support movement that financial support came more often from plant gate and shopfloor collections than from union treasuries. When $200,000-plus a year, UFCW International President Bill Wynn condemned the "Adopt-A-Family" program in a letter to AFL-CIO officers and affiliates just before Thanksgiving 1985, rank-and-file participation in this program took on a very oppositional character. The Machinists' Union (IAM) President William Winpisinger (long considered a "progressive" within organized labor) was one of the first international presidents to endorse Wynn's strictures and try to enforce them within his own organization. When the Minneapolis-St. Paul Northwest Airlines IAM Lodge voted to send $10,000 to adopt several families, Winpisinger intervened. He claimed the authority to oversee any local expenditures greater than small change and refused to allow this gesture of solidarity. Under the prodding of an aggressive and imaginative shop steward who was active in the Twin Cities P-9 Support Committee, the local lodge convened an "emergency" meeting and paid out a constitutionally required $35 per diem to everyone in attendance. There was no other business to conduct. As the meeting adjourned, rank-and-filers lined up to sign over their individual checks to P-9. The total—over $10,000!

Increasingly, rank-and-file solidarity activists formed organizations independent of the AFL-CIO in order to better support the efforts of Local P-9. Over the course of the struggle, 42 independent "P-9 support committees" were organized around the country. They played an important role—in raising funds, in promoting the boycott, and in dealing with their own local labor establishments. These labor committees also furthered cross-union communications at a local, rank-and-file level, and even linked labor activists to progressives in other movements. On occasion, they went beyond their express purpose of support for P-9 to organize support for a group of workers in their own region who were also engaged in conflict. These networks could also be extended beyond single states to establish regional levels of rank-and-file cooperation. In spring 1986, for instance, the Twin Cities P-9 Support Committee organized a food caravan with the support committees of Madison and Milwaukee, Wisconsin. We intended not only to bring food to the strikers, but to experiment with these new forms of independent labor organization and show that it could be done.

Between June and December 1985, union activists from around the country who shared a commitment to Local P-9 came together to organize "National Rank-and-file Against Concessions" (NRFAC). More than 600 official delegates convened in Chicago in December to turn the rapidly evolving network into a formal organization. Delegates not only met in intense sessions, but also walked the picket lines at the *Chicago Tribune.* Unfortunately, this new organization was quickly dominated by a sectarian left group—the Communist Labor Party (CLP). CLP members were secretly behind many of the efforts to build the National Rank-and-File Against Concessions. With their own tiny but well-placed network as a skeleton, they sought to construct a national organization that they could control. It was never clear what they intended to do with this organization, however, other than to promote the careers within the labor hierarchy of their individual members—a shipbuilder here, a steelworker there, a longshoreman somewhere else. Yet, the secretive CLPers had positioned themselves to control the organization, limit its agenda, and manipulate its network. The convention was a disaster, as activists chafed under the heavy-handedness of the CLPers, and the new organization shrivelled over the next months—just when P-9 most needed the help.

The CLP thus derailed a very promising initiative outside of the stultifying rigidity of the AFL-CIO. NRFAC tapped into healthy, energetic feelings stirred up by P-9. Labor activists catalyzed by their involvement in support for P-9 sought to build a national network capable of backing all local struggles that might block the freely falling labor standards. This, unfortunately, did not come to pass.

The CLP's brand of "labor solidarity" was not atypical of much of the Leninist left. Many groups who claimed to be "supporting" P-9 frequently harmed or limited the struggle. There were some exceptions, of course. The Fourth Internationalist Tendency and Socialist Action, in particular, offered some constructive help. But, all too often, Leninist groups placed the furtherance of their own agendas and the confirmation of their theories ahead of the expansion of P-9's struggle for union democracy and an end to concessions.

The Socialist Workers Party (SWP) is perhaps the best example. It was very vocal in its promotion of P-9, but functioned mainly to the detriment of the struggle. Among the volunteer lawyers who helped on the many legal fronts were several SWPers. Their influence was a conservative one. The lawyers advised Guyette and Winkels to lay low and avoid taking responsibility for mass actions, which contributed to an air of chaos at critical points. Twin Cities SWPers also became known for coming to meetings to argue points and vote on tactics, but then not show up to do the hard work necessary to implement those tactics. The SWP also largely held back from sharing its national and international network with the P-9ers, although they were eager to add the P-9ers' new contacts to *their* lists.

The SWP seemed to believe that little could be done to dislodge the leadership of the labor movement or to reform the movement as a whole. Their idea of "radical" activity then, barely went beyond selling their newspaper, *The Militant,* or holding an occasional "educational" event in which a speaker pointed out the "connections" between events in the United States and those in Central America or southern Africa. In an ironic way, their own behavior—so limited in what it offered—helped fulfill their prophecies. This became clearest when, led by national political committee member Mac Warren, they sought to scuttle a national rank-and-file meatpackers' conference in May 1987. If they couldn't control it, they wanted to make sure it would be ineffectual.

The failure of P-9 and its solidarity movement to fully overcome organized labor's unwillingness to support the struggles of its own most militant and creative labor activists, or overcome the obstacles caused by the "help" offered by the much of Leninist left, are serious problems. These failures helped undermined P-9's ultimate success. Yet, it would be a huge mistake to diminish the incredible level of creativity and solidarity inspired by this struggle, both in Austin and throughout the rest of the country. The P-9 solidarity movement helped surmount obstacle after obstacle. For example, when the UFCW frontally attacked Local P-9 and put it into trusteeship in June 1986, the Austin United Support Group became the very center of the struggle. They rented a new office, maintained the food shelf, accepted contributions that would have been derailed by the UFCW if sent directly to the union, promoted the Hormel boycott, and published the *Support Report* as the main vehicle of communications. Had it not been for them, the trusteeship would have ended the struggle altogether. Spouses, children, retired parents, neighbors, and friends joined P-9 members and a far-flung national support network in an impressive effort to secure victory against the combined forces of the company, the bank, the media, the state at all levels, the international union, the leadership of other unions, and the AFL-CIO.

Chapter 5

Counter-Attack and Defeat

Employers and their political allies demonstrated in the 1980s that they no longer wished to participate in the "social contract" they had helped to construct with labor from the 1930s through the 1950s. International competition, declining profit rates, greed, and ideology inspired corporate leaders to turn on unions viciously. They were willing to tolerate only those unions which agreed to act not as advocates for their members, but as agents for the corporate agenda—by accepting concessions and job reductions and by promoting union-management cooperation in place of an adversarial relationship.

It is not the least bit surprising then that the Hormel Company opposed Local P-9's campaign to maintain its living standards—both in the pay packet and in its position in the workplace. Towards local unions like P-9 which resisted this corporate drive, corporations and their representatives in government unleashed an anti-union juggernaut not seen in U.S. industrial life since the "open shop drive" of the early 20th century. Under these conditions, employers frequently drove workers to strike by making sweeping demands for economic concessions and changes in work rules, job descriptions, and on-the-job union protections that threatened to strip workers of their dignity and self-respect. When—or if—they struck, corporations then carted in "permanent replacements," essentially firing workers for exercising their once widely recognized right to strike. Judges routinely issued injunctions limiting picketing—the number of picketers, where they could stand, what they could say or do—so as to effectively gut this right as well. The forces of order—local and state police, even the National Guard—enforced these court orders and escorted strike-breakers through picket lines with ease.

One reason Hormel felt it could win a strike was that it had already decided before the strike to shift much of its production away from fresh pork to the "high value-added" end of the industry, typified by microwave-ready products, and to fish and poultry. The acquisition of catfish farms, the "Chicken by George" line, and Jenni-O Turkey, together with the expensive advertising campaign for the Top Shelf and New Traditions lines, suggest where Hormel was going. Yet, Hormel was—and remains—a major pork producer, and it was actually the company's ability to get its pork output from other plants that strengthened its hand during the strike. First, there were Hormel's other plants in the midwest and the south. Though most were unionized, they continued to produce during the strike, in some cases at visibly increased levels, including overtime. With contract expiration dates out of sync, and an international union unsympathetic to the Austin situation, little effort was made to disrupt or limit this production—until P-9's "unsanctioned" roving pickets in late January 1986. Furthermore, Hormel strengthened its hand by entering into an "exclusive marketing relationship" (later an outright acquisition) with FDL Foods, which added three more substantial pork processing plants to its system. Although the Austin plant was indeed the "flagship" plant and the most modern plant Hormel owned, they barely missed the production, even after months on strike.

The P-9ers, particularly the oldest generation, had hoped that the Hormel Foundation would come to their assistance. In the late 1940s, the Hormel family had created the Foundation and given it control over their stock. The Foundation was supposed to act in the "best interests of the Austin community." In return, the Foundation received an unusual—and very favorable—tax status within the state of Minnesota. Over the years, it was run by retired Hormel executives as well as current management. It also incorporated representatives of the local charitable community, who sat on the board while their organizations received sizeable grants. By 1985, the Foundation still held 46 percent of the stock and still enjoyed its unique tax status. Some P-9ers —especially those who remembered the paternalism of the Hormel family—expected the Foundation to dissuade the company from the course it had chosen.

They could not have been more wrong. Not only was the Foundation unwilling to play any such role, it became a tool in the hands of corporate management to control the behavior of local charitable organizations—the Mower County Mental Health Clinic, St. Olaf Hospital, the Salvation Army, and the like. The Foundation was the major donor to most of these organizations, and representatives of corporate management sat on their boards.

Hormel's tentacles reached deeply into these community institutions and provided them with powerful tools to turn against the strikers. The Mower County Mental Health Clinic decried the strike as a source of "stress" in the community, and its director launched a virtual back-to-work campaign complete with "Ray Rogers Must Go" billboards around Austin. St. Olaf Hospital refused to release any information on injuries in the Hormel plant to the media. The Mower County Food Shelf initially turned away strikers' families who sought assistance, forcing them to travel to Rochester, more than 50 miles away. Even the local churches refrained from criticizing Hormel. Oddly, some of those who proclaimed their "neutrality" were willing to house National Guardsmen sent to Austin to break P-9's picket lines. Many P-9ers were amazed that they got more support from outside their community than from within it, as they learned a compelling lesson about the nature of a "company town."

Other local institutions also served Hormel. There was the daily newspaper (the "Hormel Herald," as P-9ers called it), the radio station, and the television station. All relied heavily on Hormel for advertising revenue. All were corporate organizations in their own right. Their "line" was clear and solid from the very start—Hormel "needed" these cuts to stay "competitive" and the community "needed" Hormel to stay alive. Sometimes, their service to the company was embarrassingly blatant, as when the radio station broadcast information to scabs about when and where to report for work when the plant reopened in January 1986. On a daily basis, these media institutions contributed to the sort of climate and "public opinion" that buttressed the Hormel Company.

The Twin Cities media—certainly more "independent" of the company than the local media—was not much better. They sensationalized the story, sought to spotlight "violence," and once they had become bored with the story, were eager to declare the struggle "over." When the national media—the *Chicago Tribune,* the *New York Times,* ABC, CBS, and NBC—got interested when the plant reopened, their slant was much the same. The P-9ers consistently found themselves swimming against "public opinion" and "their community."

A key company supporter was the First Bank System (FBS). Their relationship with the Hormel Company dated from 1927. Over the ensuing years, the two institutions had frequently interlocked directors and enjoyed a particularly close relationship. FBS had also become one of the midwest's major banking systems, growing rapidly in the favorable climate of the late 1970s and early 1980s. In 1985, it controlled 16 percent of Hormel's stock, second only to the Foundation, and shared three directors with the company. According to Ray Rogers' research, FBS also was a significant player in several other regional meatpacking companies, including those who had driven wages and benefits down in the early 1980s.

FBS was pulled directly into the conflict from the outset by Rogers' strategy, which targeted them as a pressure point. P-9 literature took aim at FBS as well as Hormel, and their banks were frequent targets for pickets and demonstrations. From downtown St. Paul and Minneapolis to small rural communities, placard-bearing P-9ers ringed banks, urged the public to "honk to show your support," and handed out leaflets asking, "Who's Behind Hormel's Cold Cuts?" FBS was also a target of two other movements at this time—the anti-apartheid movement, over their sale of krugerands, and the farmers' movement, over their role in foreclosures and auctions. Thus, the campaign against the bank helped underpin P-9's coalitions outside the labor movement. It also seemed to enjoy considerable public sympathy. After the regional NLRB cited P-9 for unfair labor practices under the "secondary boycott" clause of the Taft-Hartley Act, further picketing and leafletting of banks was enjoined.

FBS, of course, remained available to Hormel throughout the struggle. It would appear that Hormel's own rich liquid assets and the unique status of the Foundation diminished its need for outside capital. But it must have been reassuring to Hormel management (Richard Knowlton, Hormel CEO, sat on FBS's board) to know that the bank's ample resources were there if needed. Moreover, FBS's continuing influence in the meatpacking industry and the role it might have played coordinating corporate support for Hormel will probably never be known, but should not be overlooked. Indeed, the more the struggle went on, the more it shed the character of a traditional labor-management conflict and assumed the trappings of a class conflict, with broad forces arrayed on both sides.

The federal government clearly chose sides in favor of manage-ment, but P-9ers still hoped for help from the local government. The mayor of Austin, Tom Kough, was himself a P-9er with nearly 30 years of seniority. He also supported the corporate campaign. But the com-pany, the media, and other politicians quickly persuaded Mayor Kough that he should see himself as a "neutral" when wearing the mayor's hat. And during the crisis of public order that hit when Hormel reopened the plant in January 1986, the police chief and the county sheriff simply excluded the mayor from their discussions with com-pany security and the state government. "Ineffectual" is not too strong a word to describe how Tom Kough played the role of mayor. Might a more forceful individual have handled the situation differently? Per-haps, but only by casting aside deep-seated ideologies about the "neutrality" of government and by standing up to a torrent of media-induced "public opinion." And, even then, his or her power would have been very limited.

The governor's office, on the other hand, held considerable power. While the AFL-CIO leadership has been eager to place the blame for the debacle of the 1980s at the feet of the Republican Party, the Hormel Strike and other major battles of the decade demonstrate that Democratic office-holders who have styled themselves as "friends of labor" are just as quick to provide corporations with the state's support as their GOP counterparts have been. This was certainly true of Governor Rudy Perpich. Perpich, a dentist by trade, was the son of a Croatian immigrant iron miner who had helped organize the Steelworkers' Union on Minnesota's Iron Range. He had built his political career within the state's Democratic Farmer-Labor Party on the symbolic currency of his ethnic, working-class roots. At the same time, Perpich typified the 1980s direction of the Demo-cratic Party, seeking to "improve" the "business climate" and make Minnesota "competitive."

In late January 1986, when Hormel reopened the plant, P-9ers and their supporters effectively—and peacefully—blocked the gates. CEO Knowlton, the police chief, the county sheriff, and even the mayor, then called on the governor to dispatch the National Guard. Perpich already had more than 300 guardsmen ready, and he ordered them into

Austin after consulting with three top labor officials—Howard Fortier of the Teamsters, Bob Killeen of the UAW, and Dan Gustafson of the Minnesota AFL-CIO.

The Guard certainly did not perceive their role as a neutral "peace-keeper" in Austin. They functioned like an occupying force, strategizing daily about P-9 as the enemy, taking whatever measures were necessary to keep the plant open. The Guard cordoned off much of Austin. Access to residential and shopping areas, as well as the plant, was restricted. Cars were stopped, drivers questioned. On I-90 in the early morning hours, state highway patrolmen rerouted all vehicles which did not have "scab permits." The Guard made it possible for Hormel to bring in its "replacements" and for P-9ers to cross their own picket lines to return to work.

The Guard's role was not only orchestrated by the governor, but was shaped by a series of Minnesota court injunctions and restraining orders that had already limited the rights of strikers in Austin. How many picketers there could be, where they could stand, what they could and couldn't do, all were limited by judicial decisions. Picketers were denied the right to take photos of scab vehicles, even though company video cameras ran constantly. Even Minnesota's 1917 "criminal syndicalism" law was dusted off, and Ray Rogers was arrested under it. One local judge even admitted that he was infringing on the First Amendment rights of the P-9ers, but said he thought the protection of "public order" necessitated such action! The "forces of order" —the local police, the county sheriff's deputies, the state police, the National Guard—all were aligned against Local P-9.

Repression came from other sources as well. The school administration in Austin decreed (with the concurrence of the Austin chapter of the Minnesota Education Association) that the strike was not to be discussed in the public schools. One high school social studies teacher with more than 20 years' seniority resigned rather than accept these conditions. P-9 parents objected to first-grade math assignments that had students count Hormel products on a sheet of paper. At the local Catholic high school, the principal was fired after he rented the gym to P-9 for a benefit basketball game against a team from the St. Paul Ford plant's UAW Local 879.

Another important source of repression came from Gary Baker and Associates, the private detective agency hired by Hormel. Baker and Associates specialized in labor conflicts, and had made quite a reputation for itself in the 1980s. P-9ers attributed much of the increase of "vandalism" in Austin to this company, and their surveillance activities contributed to an atmosphere of terror. I learned, for instance, that they had investigated me—my credit, driving, and criminal record, my occupation, my mortgage, my wife—and then had concluded that, through my relationship with Vernon Bellecourt of the American Indian Movement, I functioned as an "agent of Kaddafi." Moreover, I was acting on behalf of "Green Party terrorists" and several "Trotsky groups." Baker and Associates turned this file over to the Austin Police Department, together with my license plate numbers.

Even the FBI and the Bureau of Alcohol, Tobacco and Firearms got into the spying game. P-9ers who went on the road to solicit funds and spread the word about their struggle were shadowed by federal and private agents. Informants and spies filed reports with little more truth value than my being an "agent of Kaddafi," all of which was duly studied by police agencies and filed away. Such information was certainly used to whip up police enthusiasm for repression of the P-9 "threat."

Local P-9's enemies went far beyond corporate America and its political toadies, however. In perhaps the biggest disappointment to the P-9 strikers, the United Food and Commercial Workers Union leadership and the entire superstructure of the AFL-CIO were instrumental in crushing P-9. In the end, their role was probably the crucial one. Had they stood with P-9, as the United Mine Workers and its labor leadership did with the Pittston miners later in the 1980s, it is entirely possible that the combined forces of Hormel and the state might have been turned aside. This was not to be.

The UFCW's leadership, and its national packinghouse division under Lewie Anderson, had set a course in the early 1980s which was bound to collide with the direction P-9 was headed under its new leadership. Buffeted by corporate buy-outs, reorganizations, takeovers, mergers, plant closings, and the restructuring of the industry through substantial technological change (such as "boxed beef") and geographical decentralization, the international union envisioned a strategy of "controlled retreat." In practical terms, this meant a willingness to accept concessions, especially at the upper end of the industry, as long as this did not threaten the international union's dues base. Not surprisingly, this often led to conflict with local unions representing those workers who were being asked—by their international union as well as their employer—to grant such concessions.

Over the first half of the 1980s, no local had been able to stand up to the corporate pressure for concessions or the international union's acquiescence. Local P-9's willingness to take a stand thus threatened the international union nearly as much as it threatened the Hormel corporation. Both the UFCW and the AFL-CIO knew that Local P-9 represented a dangerous example for other labor activists and rank-and-file unionists. P-9 quickly came to symbolize democracy and membership participation, a willingness to oppose corporate demands for concessions, regardless of international union agendas or strategies, and a form of "horizontal" solidarity that threatened the vertical, bureaucratic hold that international unions exercised over their locals. As thousands of workers poured into Austin to express their support, we likened their experience to "catching a virus" from P-9. But the UFCW and the AFL-CIO were determined to prevent the spread of this virus.

How far were they willing to go? As far as they had to, it seems. As the chapter on the revitalization of P-9 showed, UFCW president William Wynn and National Packinghouse Division Director Lewie Anderson openly opposed the campaign against Hormel from the very start. They tried to isolate Jim Guyette and depicted P-9 as a "go-it-alone" rebel local. Yet, when P-9ers voted by more than 90 percent to strike in August 1985, the international had little choice but to grant official sanction and approve strike benefits of $45 a week. The UFCW leadership continued behind the scenes, however, to undermine the strike, with the frequent collusion of other labor leaders. The strike's character as "rank-and-file" vs. "leadership" was clear. And the willingness of the leadership to let P-9 lose (perhaps even their *desire* to let P-9 lose) was equally clear.

Twice in the fall of 1986, the Minnesota AFL-CIO leadership and UFCW Region 13 sought to undermine food caravans being organized by the Twin Cities P-9 Support Committee. They contacted local unions and discouraged them from contributing, urging instead that they send cash to Region 13's office in the Twin Cities. As we have seen, Wynn also sent telegrams to international union presidents around the country, urging them to discourage their locals from participating in other support programs, claiming that the money would go to Ray Rogers.

The UFCW went further. Lewie Anderson and Region 13 Director Joe Hansen met secretly with retired P-9 business agent (and Guyette opponent) Dick Schaefer and leaders of the "P-10" dissident faction, even while the strike still had the official sanction of the international union. Such meetings went on both before and after the "P-10ers" chose to cross their own picket lines. In fact, the very week that the National Guard took up its positions, Lewie Anderson appeared on Ted Koppel's "Nightline" television show to undermine Jim Guyette and support the minority anti-strike faction in P-9.

The UFCW also sought to limit the effectiveness of the campaign against Hormel. When P-9ers visited other plants, UFCW officials and local officers frequently intervened and tried to prevent communications. President Wynn had explicitly ruled out a boycott of Hormel products or extending the strike to other plants when he had granted strike sanction in August 1985, and he continued to hold firm to these positions. When P-9 sent roving pickets on its own to Ottumwa and Fremont, and hundreds of workers were fired for honoring these lines, Wynn offered no resistance to Hormel, saying that they were within their contract rights. Instead, he heaped blame on Rogers and Guyette.

Ironically, one of the tools in the UFCW's efforts to crush P-9 was the Communist Party (CP). Hormel vice president and chief henchman, Charles Nyberg claims to this day that he and CEO Richard Knowlton saved Austin from "communism" by defeating P-9. Yet, the best known "left" organization in the United States helped defeat P-9! The Communist Party sided with the UFCW and opposed P-9 as soon as the split between the local and the international became apparent. In particular, they were instrumental in developing a cover story for the UFCW attack against P-9 that could be sold to progressive elements in the labor movement who did not have firsthand contact with P-9. The CP argued that P-9 had "broken solidarity" with the Hormel chain, that they had opted to "go it alone" when they thought they had the upper hand, and now they wanted other workers to risk all for the preservation of P-9's privileges. These arguments—all forms of the "big lie" for those who had been to Austin—were circulated in the pages of the *Daily World* and picked up by the UFCW and used extensively to their advantage.

Most influential of all in this propaganda war was a widely circulated paper written by Lance Compa, which took the "big lie" to the level of "grand theory" and accused P-9 of "enterprise unionism." Compa's influence with organizations like the National Lawyers Guild and the Labor Research Association in New York City helped undermined P-9's efforts to gain solidarity among some segments of the U.S. Left. In the best tradition of propaganda, the CP's efforts did not have to convince a soul of the correctness of the UFCW's posture. They needed only to place some doubt in people's minds, especially people who had no direct contact with P-9. The CP did this on behalf of a style of business unionism that they felt most comfortable working in and to protect their members within the ranks of the UFCW's staff.

The worst UFCW betrayals were yet to come, however. On March 14, 1986, Wynn ordered P-9 to call off the strike and offer an "unconditional" return to work. More than 800 P-9ers met and, after discussion, voted overwhelmingly to ignore that order. Supporters around the country pledged to boycott Hormel products and to continue to support P-9. In early April, thousands of supporters streamed into Austin for several days of plant gate demonstrations and a major rally. On April 11, police and sheriff's deputies lobbed tear gas into a large crowd assembled for a rally (in violation of injunctions) at the plant gates. Seventeen were arrested on "felony riot" charges. Rogers and Guyette were charged with "aiding and abetting a riot" for having "mailed posters and leaflets" inviting supporters to Austin.

After this blatant attempt at legal intimidation, Wynn, Anderson, and the UFCW began to lay their plans to place P-9 in trusteeship and remove the democratically elected local leadership. On April 14, the UFCW convened a trusteeship hearing in Minneapolis. It was closed to the public. The room was small, and most of the seats were taken by UFCW staffers. The hearing examiner (a UFCW official from Texas) restricted all testimony and evidence to one question: Did P-9 disobey the UFCW order to call off the strike on March 14?

On May 8, the UFCW announced that it was taking over P-9 through trusteeship. The next day, Judge Devitt granted the international a restraining order, which limited P-9's ability to receive or disburse funds. On June 5, armed with another one of Judge Devitt's court orders, Region 13 director Joe Hansen took control of P-9's office, assisted by two deputy trustees, both of whom had been voted out of office in their own locals due to their endorsement of employer demands for concessions. The trustees then insisted that all strike and boycott activity cease. They demanded that all P-9ers remove buttons and bumper stickers, and even went to the post office to lay claim to all P-9 mail, including items addressed personally to Jim Guyette. They summarily fired P-9's two secretaries and told Guyette, Winkels, and Financial Secretary Kathy Buck (the three full-time officers) that they were fired. (The UFCW would later contest their unemployment claims, contending that they had been fired for "just cause.") The trustees expelled the retirees' organization and the United Support Group from the Austin Labor Center and closed down the food shelf. They also began legal proceedings to attach the support group's funds.

The trustees informed Hormel that the strike was over and the union was making an "unconditional" offer of a return to work. The UFCW sent a mailing to local unions across the United States, urging the purchase of Hormel products, "made by union brothers and sisters, earning the best wages and benefits in the industry." The mailing included a bright yellow sticker to be put inside vending machines (where it could not be scratched over or removed), which read "Hormel products are union made." Wynn personally appealed to union officials not to contribute to P-9's legal defense fund (for the two dozen felony offenses and hundreds of misdemeanors), on the grounds that the money might be used to sue the UFCW. The trustees also sandblasted the 16-by-80-foot mural that had been painted by more than 100 rank-and-filers on the Labor Center's brick wall. No union tradesman in town would do the job, so the trustees did the dirty work themselves. Fittingly, Austin building tradesmen picketed them while they did it.

Early in the fall of 1986, the trustees signed a contract with Hormel that granted management every concession it had sought—an expiration date out of sync with the rest of the chain, management control over work rules, a shift from plant-wide to departmental seniority, the loss of the 52 week lay-off notice, the loss of the guaranteed annual wage, the gutting of the grievance procedure, and a limit on the role of arbitrators. Nothing in the agreement addressed the safety issues which had loomed so large in the strike. Not one of the strikers (other than the

450 who had crossed the sanctioned picket lines in January and February) was returned to work.

The UFCW and Hormel had boxed the strikers in. All workers—except for those already discharged for "misconduct" and those pressured to retire—were placed on a "preferential recall list." The contract included a "Ray Rogers clause"—a promise not to promote a boycott of Hormel products and not to handbill any business that does business with Hormel. Violation of this clause was grounds for termination—including termination from the "preferential recall list." Dozens received letters from the company warning them to remove "Boycott Hormel" stickers from their cars. Some were even stopped by the local police and given similar recommendations.

The international union had done more then "sell out" this remarkable local union. It had actively collaborated with the company and the courts to crush it out of existence. After it had forced P-9ers on the recall list to take "withdrawal cards" from the union, it "returned" the local to "democratic" control. John Anker and John Morrison, both of whom had been among the first to cross the sanctioned picket lines, both of whom had been in touch with Lewie Anderson and Dick Schaefer throughout the strike, were elected president and secretary-treasurer.

While enthusiasm waned considerably after the UFCW took over the union and signed a contract with Hormel, the strikers and their supporters did not give up quietly. Hundreds of P-9ers continued their struggle, primarily by promoting the boycott of Hormel products—though they knew that such activity could lead to their being stricken from the recall list. Some activists sought to decertify the UFCW and organize a new union, the North American Meat Packers Union (NAMPU). They even ran a brief organizing drive at a packing plant in Texas. Many left town and sought work elsewhere. Some of them have emerged as union activists in other industries and in other cities. A significant group held on, kept their places on the recall list, and waited to return to work. By the summer of 1992, nearly 400 of the strikers had returned to work. According to the latest reports, they are organizing an opposition slate to challenge Morrison and Anker for control of the local.

Supporters too have shifted gears but kept up their activism. The Austin United Support Group maintained an office for two years after the strike ended, and activists from their ranks continue to organize a picnic every August to commemorate the anniversary of the strike. The Twin Cities P-9 Support Committee folded its tents, but many of its activists have helped to organize the St. Paul Labor Speakers Club, which puts on a public educational program on the last Monday night of every month, reaching hundreds of local activists. The Speakers Club has also served as the nerve center for the revival of a St. Paul Labor Day Picnic, which has attracted 4,000 to 6,000 adults and children since 1988. Other activists in other cities tell similar stories.

Indeed, activists from the various support committees have continued to struggle within their unions for the P-9 agenda: union democracy and resistance to concessions. P-9 supporters have figured prominently in Teamsters for a Democratic Union (TDU) and the New Directions Movement in the UAW, as well as in efforts to revive militant unionism in the rail, steel, and longshore industries and to promote the concept of an independent labor party. Other P-9 supporters have taken up the task of organizing clerical workers in traditionally non-unionized workplaces. Still others are attempting to build better bridges with environmental, peace and justice, and farm activists, especially around the issue of free trade with Canada and Mexico.

Despite these impressive continued efforts on the part of P-9ers and their supporters, there is no denying that the strike itself was lost. Despite their militancy and spirit, and despite the network of solidarity that supported them, the P-9ers were no match for the combined forces of the corporations, mass media, government, and business unionism that allied against them.

For many, the defeat is the only lesson drawn from the struggle of Local P-9 against Hormel. This view is perhaps most clearly visible in the Academy Award-winning documentary *American Dream* by Barbara Koppel. One scene sums up the whole thrust of the movie. In it, Ray Rogers is being interviewed by two labor reporters, Bill Serrin of the *New York Times* and James Warren of the *Chicago Tribune*. The interview took place within days after the international union called off the strike and issued an unconditional offer to return to work. Incredulous, Serrin asks Rogers: "Do you mean to say that if this strike ends and no one gets his job back, you'll still declare it a victory?" Rogers responds: "However this turns out, there has been something very positive here…" Both reporters shake their heads in disagreement and disbelief.

There is clearly a struggle to control the memory of the Hormel strike, to tame it and defame it, to convince all rank-and-filers and their supporters that any such effort would inevitably end in disaster. The UFCW has attempted to control the "official memory" of the strike by blasting the workers' mural off the Austin Labor Center wall and by manipulating the labor press and communication within the labor movement. The mass media has done it in how they have reported the story to the general public and even labor "allies" such as Barbara Koppel often tell a distorted and disempowering story.

As a historian and a first-hand observer, I have tried to show that "something very positive" did indeed happen in Austin, Minnesota, in the mid-1980s. Whatever their failures and defeats, the P-9 strikers were able to win their dignity and self-respect. They developed empowering organizing skills, built a movement culture, and developed a critical awareness of the social forces arrayed against America's working people, including the moribund labor movement itself. They also inspired thousands of people to active support across the country and, perhaps most importantly, showed what a revitalized labor movement might look like. At its best, Local P-9 presented the powers-that-be with the "threat of a good example."

The key lesson of this struggle is not that a new rank-and-file unionism is doomed to inevitable failure. Rather, it is that the new wave of unionism represented by the P-9 strikers and their supporters is necessary for the revitalization of the labor movement but is not yet sufficiently developed. The strategic and tactical issues raised by P-9's successes as well as its failures are thus at the very heart of any serious discussion about the future of the U.S. labor movement.

Part III

Looking Forward

Chapter 6

The Future
of the Labor Movement

The most disconcerting—and, unfortunately, the most common—reaction that viewers have had to Barbara Koppel's documentary *American Dream* is to want to distance themselves from the labor movement. They come away from the film seeing the labor movement as depressingly mired in internal conflicts and confusion, hopelessly trapped in a downward spiral. Though their anger toward corporate and government behavior may increase, they see no light at the end of the tunnel. And so they turn away from the labor movement and, at best, choose to put all their energies into other movements, and, at worst, become increasingly convinced that progressive social change is impossible.

This book is intended not just to "set the record straight," or to reach labor activists with the "lessons" of the Hormel Strike, but to urge social activists to reconsider the labor movement and their relationship to it. This is not grounded in abstract faith or Marxist imperative, but in a reading of history, both distant and recent, and in using that reading of history to peer into the future.

The U.S. labor movement has developed in fits and starts, rather than by a simple linear progression. Each of the leaps forward came on the heels of periods of decline and crisis and brought with it qualitative as well as quantative change. New and different kinds of people joined; new and different kinds of organizations appeared; and new and different kinds of strategies and tactics are employed.

These periods of renewal do not spontaneously emerge out of thin air. They are prefigured, prepared for, and nourished by years of struggle, much of which, initially, appeared fruitless. Yet, when the leaps began, it was activists from these prior years of struggle who led the way, and rank-and-filers who had begun to feel empowered who now made their mark on history. And, typically, it was the leaders of the existing, but declining, organizations who bitterly opposed these new breakthroughs, often with more venom than the employers and public officials who were being challenged.

We need to understand this historical pattern in order to sketch the contours of the future of the labor movement and figure out what kinds of roles we can play. My point in what follows is not by any stretch of the imagination to provide a comprehensive history of the development of the U.S. labor movement. Rather, I want to sketch out a historical pattern of development by leaps, and sort out the dynamics that underlie each of them. I also want to employ this approach to the 1980s, including the Hormel Strike, in order to peer beyond history into the future.

The first great leap in the development of the U.S. labor movement came in the 1820s and 1830s. It was largely made by the sons of the revolutionary generation, young and middle-aged artisans who saw the industrial revolution undermining the goals of the revolution of 1776. They found the economic independence valued by their fathers and mothers ever more elusive, as they faced a life of wage-labor rather than self-employment. Journeymen artisans had been organizing craft unions since before the American Revolution. These unions had rarely drawn a sharp line between journeymen (wage earners) and masters (employers), since most journeymen expected to become masters later on in life. But this pattern began to break down in the late 18th century, as more and more journeymen found themselves facing a life of permanent wage-labor. With the increasing division of labor, the emergence of the cottage, or putting-out system, and the appearance of factories, traditional expectations seemed less and less likely to be realized.

The decade of 1810-1820 proved to be a disaster for the younger generation of journeymen. First the War of 1812 and then the depression of 1819 disrupted economic activity, threw many out of work, and forced them to consume the savings they had been putting aside to take that big step toward self-employment and economic independence. The existing unions (many of them led by masters) proved useless as a means of self-defense.

As discussions moved beyond self-defense toward social change, journeymen began building new kinds of organizations. Their primary vehicles were "trade unions" (multi-craft, horizontally-based local bodies) and "workingmen's parties" (local, independent political formations). Both types of organizations were grounded in horizontal solidarity, linking all journeymen in a given city or community in order to have an impact on local economic policies and practices. In some areas, they also included the first generation of factory workers, most of whom were young women, and they incorporated their demands about controlling the length of the working day and guaranteeing safe conditions on the job.

Over the course of the 1820s and 1830s, this new labor movement shook the emerging power structure. From the big cities of Boston and Philadelphia to the smaller, industrializing communities of New England and the Middle Atlantic states, there were "general" strikes and "reform tickets." There were even efforts to link up these local movements into regional and national organizations.

Employer opposition, political chicanery, growing concern about slavery, uneven economic development, and a major economic depression in the later 1830s ultimately undermined this new movement. But it had left its mark on the still young U.S. working class, and its activists would continue to figure prominently in the evolution of the labor movement over the next generation. Their experiences and ideas would infuse the rebuilt craft unions, local central labor bodies, and the efforts to create national unions and national federations of unions.

A half-century would pass, however, before there would be another leap forward for the U.S. labor movement. It came in response to the rise of producers' goods industries, such as rail, coal mining, and steel; the emergence of corporations as the most important form of business organization; the appearance of "robber barons" as a qualitatively new generation of the rich and powerful; and the formation of a genuinely national economy, constructed by railroad networks, financial networks (via banks), and an increasingly centralized national political system. Again, the leap forward followed on the heels of a period of deep economic difficulty, the depression of 1873-1878. And, again, the leap followed the failure of the then existing labor organizations to mount an effective response.

Once again, the activists represented a new social layer and coalesced around new experiences. Many of them were Irish or German immigrants or the children of immigrants. Though most of them were skilled workers, few were journeymen artisans. Rather, they worked in the new factories and industries of the era. Out of their experiences there emerged a vision of cooperation, of collective betterment rather than individual independence. As before, most of the activists were men and most were white, but more than ever before, some were black and some were women. These activists put their energies into the creation of a new organization, the Knights of Labor (KOL). At its base, the KOL consisted of "local assemblies," most of which—in contrast to the craft-based trade unions—had members from a variety of occupations. In each city or community, these local assemblies were then linked into "district assemblies." Every year, delegates from these district assemblies met for a "general assembly," to set the policies for the organization as a whole. This structure was grounded in horizontal solidarity, and it functioned effectively to provide strike support, to organize producers' cooperatives, and to launch independent labor political parties.

The KOL swept the United States in the mid-1880s. Eighty percent of all counties in the country had at least one local assembly. Well over one million joined, though, with a high turnover rate, not everyone belonged all at once. In many places, KOL-based political parties gained control of city government, or at least shook up entrenched power. Producers' cooperatives mushroomed, particularly in industries that required little capital to enter. The KOL was the first labor organization in this country to make a concerted effort to include the unskilled as well as the skilled, women as well as men, immigrants as well as the native born, and workers of color as well as whites.

The still young American Federation of Labor (born in 1881 as the Federation of Organized Trades) was one of the KOL's most bitter opponents. The craft-based unions affiliated with the AFL urged skilled workers to stick together to protect their privileges, especially within those industries which were still relatively stable, rather than participate in a movement to challenge the entire political and economic system. More than a few unionists were unsure, and joined both organizations. But the AFL's opposition undermined the KOL, especially when the employers, the government, and the media launched their attack.

The KOL had ridden the cresting wave of the Eight Hour Movement. By 1886, it had become a serious threat to the agendas of business developers and their political allies. On May 1, more than 400,000 workers went on strike for a shorter workday. Leaders of the movement sought to expand the strike, especially to the masses of unskilled workers employed in large factories. The focus of attention became the McCormick Harvester Works in Chicago, at that time the largest factory in the world. KOL strike leaders rallied daily outside the plant, urging the workforce of newly arrived southern and eastern European immigrants to join them.

On May 4, this effort literally exploded. When police sought to break up a rally (for lack of a permit), someone threw a bomb into the ranks of the police. They responded by opening fire on the crowd. When the smoke cleared, there were casualties on both sides, and the leaders of Chicago's movement were in jail, charged with murder. This opened the door to a wholesale attack on the KOL by employers, local governments, and the newspapers. They were vilified as proponents of violent revolution, and they were confronted with stiff repression from one end of the country to the other.

Momentum soon shifted, and the KOL entered a period of decline nearly as precipitous as its rise had been meteoric. In less than two years, 90 percent of the organization's membership had lapsed. Many skilled workers turned to the trade unions of the AFL. Some did this as a gesture of defeat, but others creatively used AFL local central labor bodies to fulfill many of the functions of KOL district assemblies. Indeed, sympathy strikes (albeit within the limits of the shared interests of skilled workers) flourished over the next two decades. But, on the whole, the Knights' agenda receded from public view, its potential unrealized.

The U.S. industrial scene remained volatile, and the labor movement's next leap came soon, soon enough that many veterans of the 1880s were still around and able to participate. It is important to recognize this development as a leap, and not simply as an extension or revival of the earlier movement. In some 20 years, a lot had changed. No word conveys these changes better than "mass"— mass production and mass immigration. Together, these developments had radically changed the make-up of the U.S. working class and the challenges its members faced. These pressures lay the basis for the next leap in the development of the labor movement.

The ideas of Frederick Winslow Taylor and Henry Ford underpinned the reorganization of production. Taylor analyzed skilled work, via techniques such as time and motion studies, in order to restructure work so as to separate its mental elements from its manual ones. This "scientific management" then sought to take the mental part of the work off the shopfloor and centralize it in the management office. Ford's mass production techniques divided manual work into ever smaller component parts, each worker to repeat the same tasks, the same motions, over and over. Industrial work thus became "deskilled" and "routinized."

At the same time, more than a half million new immigrants poured into industrial America every year. They came from southern and eastern Europe, where they had been farmers, farm laborers, or casual laborers. Few had industrial experience. They came to America in pursuit of unskilled wage-labor opportunities, and they arrived at a time when mass industry had a seemingly unquenchable demand for the labor power they had to offer. With low living standards and expectations hatched in impoverished conditions in Europe, they eagerly grabbed at even the low wages and dangerous jobs that U.S. industrialists offered them.

The craft-based trade unions of the AFL showed little, if any, interest in these new workers. Union leaders typically saw them as "unorganizable." They didn't speak English, seemed willing to work for low wages, had little sense of "rights," and appeared deferential to authority. They were very different from the skilled workers of northern and western European backgrounds who largely made up the membership of the AFL.

These union leaders did not even seem particularly concerned that the new immigrants made up the workforce in the rapidly growing industries of mass production, while their own membership remained on the shrinking island of small-scale production. They felt that their skills, their cooperative relationship with some business leaders in organizations such as the National Civic Federation, and their friendship with some politicians could preserve their privileges.

But mass production and mass immigration set the pace for the entire economy, and it increasingly ate away at the AFL's privileged island. Scientific management undercut the power of skilled workers inside the factories, such as machinists, molders, boilermakers, butchers, and tool and die makers, while mass produced goods crowded hand-made products out of consumer markets. In the early 1900s, employers launched an "open shop drive" to push unions off what remained of their island, and a depression in 1907 further imperilled workers' jobs and lives.

These changes and challenges laid the basis for the next leap in the development of the labor movement—the Industrial Workers of the World (IWW). In 1905, veteran activists came together in Chicago to establish this new organization. Though it would languish for its first few years, by 1909 it had begun to shake the centers of industrial power across America.

The IWW consciously sought to organize the unskilled segment of the workforce, from migratory harvest hands to factory workers. It emphasized a new structure, the industrial union, which differed from both the craft unions of the AFL and the local assemblies of the KOL. The industrial union seemed an appropriate form for the mass factory workforces, which had only recently been created. While the IWW emphasized organizational unity, it celebrated the cultural diversity of the immigrant workforce, publishing literature in more than a dozen languages, and employed cartoons, songs, poems, and plays. It also introduced new strategies and tactics, from sabotage ("the conscious withdrawal of efficiency") to the "general strike." Its anthem, "Solidarity Forever," gave voice to its vision of a unified working class able to transform industrial society.

The IWW spread rapidly, from the mines and steel mills to the harvest fields, docks, textile mills, and mass production factories. Its members used it to improve their immediate conditions and to look forward to broad social change. Here was a creative response to the challenges posed by the new terms of industrial life in America in the early 20th century.

World War I gave employers and the government the excuse they sought to destroy the IWW. State after state passed "criminal syndicalism" legislation, outlawing not merely the IWW but the very ideas they represented. Immigrant workers were threatened with deportation and accused of "disloyalty." After the war, vigilante groups launched wholesale attacks on IWW offices, organizers, and even rank-and-file members. By the early 1920s, the IWW had largely been destroyed as an effective organization. But, as with earlier movements, its ideas and activists lived on, ready to play an important role when the next historic leap emerged.

The next leap came at what was, up to that point, the bleakest period in U.S. labor history—the Great Depression. The "Crash" of 1929 and the ensuing industrial depression brought mass unemployment, reduced hours, wage cuts, deteriorating working conditions, and a new insecurity to U.S. workers. Yet, the labor movement had been in a crisis for a decade before the Depression even began. Unions had already declined from a peak of five million members in 1919 to barely two and one-half million in 1929. The most rapidly growing industries —mass production—remained thoroughly non-union. As the depression conditions worsened in the early 1930s, the existing unions offered little resistance.

The tide began to turn in 1933 (though unemployment was at its worst), as veteran activists took advantage of an improving political climate and a deepening rank-and-file frustration to launch militant local organizing campaigns. These campaigns emphasized the horizontal solidarity of the Knights of Labor and the industrial unionism of the IWW, and they brought veterans of these earlier movements together with the children of immigrants, who expected America to provide them with an improved lifestyle. These organizing campaigns further refined the structure of industrial unionism and employed a new tactic, the sitdown strike, which enabled activists to shut down production without being forced into hand-to-hand combat against their unemployed friends and neighbors or be "locked out" of their factories by the employers.

The leaders of the AFL bitterly opposed these developments. They red-baited the activists, forbid them to organize industrial unions, accused them of "dual unionism," and even organized scabs against them. Due to their resistance, union activists in most cases stepped outside the AFL to build new organizations which, in 1935, became the Congress of Industrial Organizations (CIO). But even the AFL unions were energized and revived, often over their own leaders' objections.

This leap transformed the labor movement and generated some significant changes in U.S. society. By World War II, nearly four million workers had joined unions affiliated with the CIO, and another four million had joined existing AFL unions. It wasn't just a question of numbers. Unions were rebuilt from the workplace on up, and they forced new concessions from industrial management. The new labor movement also generated pressures on the federal government. This resulted in the passage of new labor laws and the creation of new programs that assured new rights and minimum conditions for most U.S. workers.

This leap was not just a reaction to the hard times of the Great Depression. It had been prefigured by the mostly unsuccessful struggles of immigrant industrial workers to organize mass production industries in the 1920s and early 1930s. It had also grown out of the maturation of a working-class culture that transcended individual ethnic sub-cultures, emphasized job security, and expressed rising expectations about the standard of living. These developments were nurtured in industrial workplaces where informal work groups had built close bonds over years of working together. As we saw in Chapter Two, this created fertile soil for veteran activists like Frank Ellis and those younger activists who, in better times, might have risen out of the working class altogether.

The leap of the 1930s, much like its historical parallels in the 1820s-30s, 1880s, and 1910s, eroded over time. Employer opposition, government repression, cooptation, and internal union bureaucratization would sap the unions' strength. While some activists remained on the scene, a new generation would come to adulthood taking unions for granted and knowing little about their origins.

This brings the labor movement, the working class—indeed all of us—up to the 1980s. We need to re-examine the 1980s in general, and the Hormel Strike in particular, for the elements within that crisis that might *prefigure* the labor movement of the future. The historical vignettes sketched earlier in this chapter direct our attention to the entrance of new groups of workers into the labor movement, the emergence of new kinds of organizations, the expression of new goals, the adoption of new tactics, and a renewed challenge to existing labor organizations.

The major growth industries of recent years are in the service sector. At the beginning of the 1980s, these were largely non-union preserves. Indeed, over the course of the decade, unions barely established beachheads in this sector. Yet, there were some very important developments in these industries. Though they received scant attention in the media, they signalled the entrance of key new groups of workers into the labor movement, new groups that may well be the instigators of the movement's next leap.

Union organization made a breakthrough in the healthcare industry, with nurses, nurses' aides, and licensed practical nurses leading the way. The year before the Hormel Strike, 6,300 members of the Minnesota Nurses Association conducted a successful five-week strike of thirteen Twin Cities hospitals. This strike represented an important transition in many nurses' thinking, from seeing themselves in "professional association" terms to conceptualizing themselves in "union" terms. They began to see collective action as a necessary underpinning for professional work, rather than as a contradiction of their sense of "professionalism." The nurses presented themselves as "experts," and they expressed their bargaining demands in terms of how they would improve patient care. Struggles at Boston City Hospital, Buffalo General Hospital, and the New York City League of Voluntary Hospitals as reported in *A Troublemaker's Handbook* suggest the Twin Cities experience was not unusual among nurses in the 1980s.

Other healthcare workers also engaged in new activism in the 1980s. Nursing homes became battlegrounds for union organizing campaigns. Creative corporate campaigns exposed the financial interests which gobbled up nursing home dollars and kept workers poor and patients poorly cared for. Some unions built effective coalitions with community organizations, especially when workers of color were involved, as with Boston City Hospital and New York City's Local 1199. In some cases, healthcare workers organized coalitions among themselves, linking up across union boundaries. In all cases, healthcare workers linked the importance of collective organization to their desire to provide the best possible patient care while they gained new dignity and self-respect through their activism.

Similar developments can be discerned in the hotel and restaurant industries, which also expanded significantly in the 1980s. Union struggles in these industries revolved around dignity issues, as well as problems of low wages and meager benefits. In Boston, Hotel Employees and Restaurant Employees (HERE) Local 26 distinguished itself by resisting the mistreatment of its members. Gaining and enforcing strong contract language against sexual harassment was a top union priority. So, too, was protection of immigrant workers' rights to wear name tags with their correct names, rather than Americanized versions picked by their supervisors. The union also opposed management directives for workers to give up mops and scrub floors on their knees, or for bell captains to give up their chairs and remain standing in hotel lobbies. Often, HERE 26 relied on mass direct action, including sit-ins in lobbies, to address what they called "class action grievances." Not only was this approach effective, but the very process empowered rank-and-file union members and gave them the very dignity they were seeking.

While the Boston local's experiences were especially notable, they were not alone in this industry. In San Francisco, HERE Local 2 employed nationally coordinated boycotts against recalcitrant hotels. In the Twin Cities, HERE Local 17 turned to peace movement veterans for help against a hostile downtown hotel. Activists from the Honeywell Project trained union officers and rank-and-filers in the techniques of civil disobedience. On Superbowl weekend in January 1992, they conducted a sit-in in the lobby of the Normandy Hotel, with the support of not only labor and peace activists, but also the American Indian Movement, which was protesting the use of racist mascots by professional sports teams. Not only did the sit-in lead to a quick and favorable settlement at the hotel, but many of the union members joined AIM activists in leafletting the Superbowl the next day!

Even though the high-tech sector of the economy remained a largely non-union preserve, significant developments are noticeable there, too. At IBM, a group called "IBM Workers United" has existed since 1976, circulating a newsletter and building an international network of communications. At the major IBM facility in Endicott, New York, its members function like stewards, organizing group actions around grievances and health and safety issues. Interestingly, IBM Workers United has remained independent of the AFL-CIO and its member unions. Its activists feel that many of their fellow workers are still skeptical of the official labor movement, and that most unions would have little patience with their organizing approach, which has been developing gradually over more than a dozen years.

There have been other breakthroughs in high-tech. In the telephone industry, at both AT&T and the regional "baby bells," unions fought effectively for workers' rights against monitoring and surveillance. Some locals employed creative direct action tactics such as "group grievances" and petitions followed up by all the signers ceasing work and marching into the labor relations office. In 1988, the Communications Workers of America (CWA) and the International Brotherhood of Electrical Workers (IBEW) jointly launched a "mobilization campaign" against NYNEX, which linked 60,000 workers spread across more than 40 locals. For ten months, the unions trained local officers, stewards, and more than 3,000 volunteer "coordinators" into an organizational network able to call on-the-job actions or sudden walkouts. Bimonthly newsletters, rallies, informational picketing, and "color days" when union members wore red T-shirts to work, bonded this new network together and involved thousands more rank-and-filers. These innovations enabled the unions to conduct a successful four-month strike in late 1989, in which they turned back NYNEX's demands for concessions.

Most of high-tech is still non-union. Some recent books—Dennis Hayes' *Behind the Silicon Curtain;* Barbara Garson's *The Electronic Sweatshop;* and Robert Howard's *Brave New Workplace*—offer plenty of reasons why this has been the case. But the experiences of "IBM Workers United" and some of these CWA locals and regional organizations also suggest that something much more encouraging is possible, something that links the pursuit of workplace dignity with empowering, participatory tactics.

Clerical workers have been at the heart of some of the most exciting developments, particularly on university campuses. It is not just that unions have won organizing drives at Harvard, Yale, the University of Minnesota, and the University of Illinois, but that new approaches to both organizing and the internal life of unions have emerged in these campaigns. These new approaches revolve around the self-conscious building of a culture which links and empowers the largely female clericals. This building process may take years, but as Toni Gilpin's *On Strike for Respect: The Yale Clerical Strike of 1984-85* shows, it prepares rank-and-filers to challenge their employers for power at the workplace, even if it takes a prolonged strike to do so.

Clerical workers who have participated in this process have proven equally unwilling to accept a bureaucratic and passive form of organization within their union. These clerical workers have been represented by different unions—AFSCME, CWA, SEIU, UAW District 65, even HERE (at Yale). They have built an effective communications network among themselves independent of these unions. Individual activists travel back and forth, visiting each other and helping with new organizing drives at other colleges, regardless of which union might be involved. They also continue to refine and articulate their distinct model.

Another example of new workers entering the labor movement and generating new kinds of organizations comes from the South. In the mid-1980s, a group called Black Workers for Justice (BWFJ) was organized in North Carolina. It linked community organizing with workplace organizing, and it infused its campaigns among some of this country's lowest paid workers with pride and empowerment. Its singing group, the Fruit of Labor, helped express its views within the context of Southern black culture, even as it opened its membership ranks to white workers. BWFJ's approach was innovative in other ways as well. Its activists helped workers organize *before* they affiliated with a particular union. This gave them a position of autonomy from which to deal with the formal structures of the labor movement. BWFJ has not yet succeeded in its expressed goal to organize the South, but it has demonstrated the most hopeful approach the labor movement has seen since the dismantling of Operation Dixie in the late 1940s.

Among other workers of color, the 1980s saw some exciting breakthroughs. The SEIU launched a creative "Justice for Janitors" campaign which challenged cleaning service sub-contractors in large cities. This campaign had an intentionally broad character, taking on a number of shops at once and pushing for immediate recognition, relying on militant direct action, such as mass picketing and street demonstrations. Organizers chose to by-pass the standard NLRB process of seeking to sign cards and force NLRB elections one shop at a time. They built upon immigrant social networks to create a new, empowered culture. The campaign's slogan, *"Si Se Puede"* (Yes, We Can!), expressed the cleaning workers' new sense of empowerment.

I do not want to give the impression that the labor movement is successfully "organizing the unorganized." As I pointed out in Chapter One, barely one union organizing drive out of four succeeded in the

1980s. But these diverse service sector "victory stories" share some important common threads, which suggest the mosaic of the labor movement of the future. These are expanding industries, whose activities cannot be shipped abroad to be performed. Nor are they subject to "foreign competition." Their workers are also representative of the fastest growing segments of the workforce, predominantly female and non-white. These successful union campaigns have rested precisely on emphasizing the particularities of these workers' experiences, as women, as immigrants, as members of communities of color, and using them as a source of collective strength and as the foundation for a culture of resistance. The very act of organizing has empowered these workers and brought them a new sense of dignity and self-respect.

New kinds of labor organization increasingly appeared throughout the 1980s. While the Hormel Strike went the furthest in this direction, other labor struggles in the 1980s showed similar dynamics. Both family support groups and local-level support committees appeared in several strikes. In the Pittston coal miners' strike in 1988-89, "The Daughters of Mother Jones" played an important role in the organization of civil disobedience, as well as support rallies and food drives. The miners also opened a "Camp Solidarity" to house the thousands of supporters who brought food caravans or just came to visit the picket lines.

In some communities, labor coalitions became fairly permanent fixtures, taking on a variety of functions. The Boston Labor Support Project and the Tompkins-Cortland (NY) Labor Coalition performed valuable strike support work. The Intercraft Association of Minnesota linked thousands of railroad workers from more than a dozen unions, through a newspaper and a series of conferences. In addition to hosting a monthly public educational program, the St. Paul (Minnesota) Labor Speakers Club helped revitalize the celebration of Labor Day and initiated an annual "Celebration of Labor and the Arts." The Youngstown (Ohio) Workers Solidarity Club organized strike support activities and served as the base for new organizations among retirees and workers concerned with environmental hazards. The list goes on and on. These were (and are) non-bureaucratic organizations, grounded in principles of democracy and solidarity, which educate and empower their rank-and-file participants.

Intensive struggle was not the only source of organizational innovation in the 1980s. Activists within some unions sought to refashion their organization's internal, day-to-day culture, around the concepts of "social unionism" and the "organizing model." Their intent was to transform their unions from within, to rescue them from the dead legacy of decades of business unionism. While their successes might have been limited, their efforts, like the other developments discussed in this chapter, could point to the future of labor organizing.

An essential ingredient of business unionism was to restrict a union's scope to the immediate economic interests of its members. In their heyday during the 1950s and 1960s, unions put on the blinders. They were not to address themselves to their members' concerns about non-workplace issues, such as housing, education, the environment, or war and peace. They were also not to address themselves to the needs and concerns of working people other than their dues-paying members. We could ironically twist Jesse Jackson's well-worn phrase: they kept their eyes on the "prize." But this "prize" was the wage and benefit packet of their members. Period.

Proponents of "social unionism" advocate the reinvolvement of unions in both their members' non-workplace issues and the needs of working people beyond the ranks of their immediate membership. They are aware that the labor movement has been historically strongest in this country when it has fought for the interests of all working people, not just union members, and when it has been a part of members' whole lives, not just their workplaces. They are also aware that recent history, the 1980s, has demonstrated that unions can no longer be successful on wage and benefit issues if they restrict their energies to this realm alone.

This new approach has provided activists with a daunting, but exciting, agenda. Some have launched projects to connect the arts—music, theater, poetry, painting—with the labor movement. Plays and songs have been written and performed for and by working people, from coast to coast. Festivals and songfests have become annual events. Popular art forms—posters, calendars, cartoons, and T-shirts—have multiplied. In some cases, individual unions or city central labor bodies have sponsored or participated in these activities.

"Social unionism" advocates have also promoted participation in coalitions with non-labor organizations. They have brought unions together with peace, homeless, environmental, farm, and justice organizations. Some of the most successful work has been done around the "conversion" issue, the transformation of defense plants from military hardware to the production of socially useful goods in such a way that workers keep their jobs and put their skills to work. Jobs With Peace coalitions around the country have brought peace activists together with labor rank-and-filers. In the late 1980s-early 1990s, discussion of the North American Free Trade Agreement brought labor activists into coalitions with farm and environmental activists. The Minnesota Fair Trade Coalition has been typical of grassroots organizations that have been generated all over this country. It links a variety of local unions with the Resource Center of the Americas, the Minnesota Farmers Union, the Clean Water Action Project, Greenpeace, Up and Out of Poverty, the Alliance of the Streets, the Catholic/Lutheran Northwestern Minnesota Rural Life Commission, the North Country Co-op, and so on.

The Free Trade Agreement has also spurred international organizing in new and exciting ways. Dozens of conferences, attended by rank-and-filers, have brought local union activists from Canada, Mexico, and the United States together. Often, these conferences have been organized without the support or even against the opposition of international unions and the AFL-CIO. Similarly, group tours to Mexico and home visits of rank-and-file workers from country to country have been organized. Through these activities, workers have penetrated stereotypes and prejudices and gotten to know each other as human beings. This provides a real foundation for international solidarity.

There have been some impressive manifestations of such solidarity. In 1989, Ford workers in Cuautitlan, Mexico, went on strike against a wage cut that their official union had accepted. They sat in and occupied the plant. Armed gunmen attacked them, killing one of them, Cleto Nigno. A year later, in January 1990, 2000 Ford workers at the St. Paul truck assembly plant wore black ribbons with Nigno's name in a demonstration demanding that Ford explain its role in this tragedy. The ribbons had been made by the Canadian Auto Workers. This demonstration linked Ford workers in all three North American countries. Similarly, a Twin Cities conference in January 1991 opened with a lively demonstration at Pillsbury headquarters in Minneapolis to protest the closing of the Green Giant vegetable processing plant in Watsonville, California, and the moving of its work to Irapuato, Mexico.

Canadian participants in the conference joined in the demonstration, again emphasizing the cross-border links of solidarity. These sorts of activities, while unable to block the North American Free Trade Agreement, do provide the experiences out of which genuinely international unions can emerge. In the future, unions grounded in solidarity can stand up to multinational corporations and defend workers' common interests. In all these ways, a new "social unionism" may set the agenda for the labor movement of the future.

Several rank-and-file activists have also promoted an "organizing model" as an alternative to the "service model" that characterizes business unionism. The "organizing model" revolves around building a communications network within and between workplaces and decentralizing the responsibility for carrying out union functions. This network functions like a circulatory system, and information—such as leaflets, newsletters, and surveys—flows like blood through it. Communication is often face-to-face rather than anonymous or impersonal. Some unions, such as the Communications Workers of America (CWA) in their struggle with the NYNEX telephone company, found it a short step to transform this network into a "mobilization" network, using it to inform workers about rallies, informational pickets, and even workfloor slowdowns. Other unions, such as the Machinists, have emphasized the concept of "one-on-one" organizing to build union identity and spirit.

It is not just that these activists prefer the "organizing model" on ideological grounds, but that the crisis of the 1980s demonstrated that the "service model" has ceased to work. When corporate management and government officials withdrew from the social contract that tied them to business unionism, the system that provided wage and benefit increases, a modicum of fairness through grievance procedures, and respect for arbitration, collapsed like a house of cards. It became clear—to some local labor activists, at least—that union members would enjoy protection and unions would enjoy respect only when they could command it once again. They realized that the term "organized" labor was a euphemism at best, and that it was time to start at square one again.

There have been a number of successful small projects in this vein. Locals of a variety of unions have initiated "solidarity funds" to support workers facing discipline for resisting overloaded jobs. Such funds have not only strengthened the resolve of rank-and-file workers on the shopfloor, but, collected face-to-face, they have counteracted some of the organizational atrophy traceable to the automatic dues check-off. Some locals have experimented with writing mission statements, usually through a process that encourages broad rank-and-file participation. The process itself—debating the meaning of terms such as "democracy," "equality," and "fairness"—is educational and empowering. Members also develop a new sense of ownership of the union's purposes, and they have a rank-and-file agenda to which they can hold their officers accountable. Another form of organizing has been the "pledge card," by which rank-and-filers promise, in the interests of strengthening the union, to participate in certain activities (rallies, shopfloor actions, informational pickets, and the like) over the course of the ensuing year. The very wording of such pledge cards (e.g., "Whereas it is not enough to belong to the union and authorize the deduction of dues from my pay check...") emphasizes empowerment.

Very few unions, to be sure, have wholeheartedly remade themselves in the image of this "organizing model." It is a lot of work, and the pressure to keep up with the daily duties and demands of the existing (though largely dysfunctional) system keeps activists from implementing a totally new strategy. But where pieces of it have been tried, activists and rank-and-filers have gotten a glimpse of what a participatory union could be like.

Both "social unionism" and the "organizing model" have represented encouraging attempts to reform the existing labor movement from within. Neither has been a raving success, and it is increasingly clear that a strategy that relies only on internal union reform is not sufficient. But it is important to view these experiments as harbingers of a future labor movement. Our experiences with them will be incorporated in the next leap the labor movement takes, a leap that will need to go beyond the limits of self-reform.

Another development in the late 1980s is best understood in these terms as well—the discussion of independent labor political organization. Tony Mazzocchi, a high-ranking national officer of the Oil, Chemical & Atomic Workers Union (OCAW), has been the prime catalyst for this discussion. He has generated an organization called Labor Party Advocates (LPA), which has taken an interesting approach to this longstanding topic within the labor movement. LPA was started off through a series of surveys of rank-and-filers in a variety of local and national unions. These surveys assessed their sense that both the Democrats and the Republicans represent a largely pro-business agenda and that working people need a political expression of their own. Consistently, rank-and-filers scored higher on these surveys than did union officeholders, a point that LPA did not shy away from stressing. Indeed, the whole survey process suggested that the higher up one was in the union hierarchy, the more likely one was to be entangled in relationships with incumbent politicians—and that rank-and-filers saw little benefit for themselves in this.

LPA launched a series of chapters, not to run candidates, but to promote the discussion of the concept and to circulate more of these surveys. Some of these chapters enjoyed the endorsement of individual local unions, but, to no one's surprise, the AFL-CIO at all levels kept its distance. Most of the chapters consisted of individual activists, and in some cities they became the sort of umbrella networks that labor support committees had been in others.

Interestingly, even within LPA, grassroots members chafed at the national leadership's reticence to initiate actual campaigns. Individual chapters urged that this step be taken, even as Mazzocchi and other national leaders recommended patience. There are also LPA members who fear that basing independent labor politics on the unions alone is too narrow, and that a broader conception is necessary to incorporate non-unionized women and workers of color as well as to reach out to activists in other movements. This whole arena of political expression remains unstable, but the debates themselves suggest that fresh thinking is going on within the ranks of the labor movement.

There has also been some fresh thinking and experimentation with new tactics of struggle. Two of the most important of these tactics have been corporate campaigns and inside strategies. Both are based on the recognition that the 1980s demonstrated that, by themselves, traditional labor tactics no longer worked. Like "social unionism" and the "organizing model," both types of action have rarely been applied as precisely as their theorists might have liked. But, again, they do give a glimpse of things to come.

The Hormel Strike brought the concept of the corporate campaign into the forefront of many labor discussions. This tactic meant careful investigation of the financial networks that stood behind the company, and then the mobilization of rank-and-file union members and their families and supporters to put pressure on key elements of those financial networks. The idea was that these elements would, in turn, put pressure on the company to settle with the union.

The corporate campaign strategy has been widely applied in a variety of situations. It has usually taken a long time to have an effect on a company's policies, often too long to make a difference in the outcome of a struggle. But it has played many constructive roles, from educating workers about the ways corporations are structured and connected with each other, to the idea of holding formerly anonymous corporate executives personally responsible for the consequences of their business decisions and actions. The corporate campaign strategy has also encouraged labor activists to think more systematically about how they communicate their message to a larger community, and how they deal with the media in particular.

More than any other traditional labor tactic, the strike was a casualty of the changed climate of the 1980s. Corporate willingness to hire "permanent replacements" and government willingness to support that decision sapped much of the effectiveness that strikes once had. Labor activists looked high and low for alternatives. Many found the notion of "inside strategies" to be appealing.

This was hardly a new idea. Indeed, the IWW had pioneered the concept under such names as "striking on the job," "working to rule," or even "sabotage." The idea was to pressure the employer by having a clear impact on output, without risking one's paycheck or job. Of course, this called for a high degree of organization at the workplace itself, often more organization than a strike required. Jerry Tucker, who developed this approach in UAW Region 5, called it "running the plant backwards."

Where "inside strategies" were most successful, they often rested on the sort of networks built in the "organizing model" discussed earlier. Typically employed after the expiration of a contract, they also relied on "concerted action" which had been restrained by the rules of grievance and arbitration procedures. A Troublemaker's Handbook recounts many examples of creative applications of this approach, such as group grievances, entire departments calling themselves a grievance committee and, therefore, stopping production to "discuss" a grievance with the labor relations people, or scrupulously following safety regulations. Yet, it is also clear that "inside strategies" were no more of a panacea than were corporate campaigns. They were also risky propositions, and employers often fired activists, either to intimidate other workers or to provoke a more traditional strike in which they could then resort to "replacement" workers. More than an alternative to the traditional strike, they were one element of the revitalization process, connected with the internal reorganization of local unions.

Another important tactical development has been the turn to civil disobedience. Hormel strikers and their supporters were the first to use it in the 1980s, but many of them admitted that they had waited until it was really too late to have an impact on the outcome of the struggle. For them, it was more an expression of moral witness than a tactic geared to effectively resisting employers and the government. But other union activists watched and learned, and as they saw the traditional tactics of the labor movement turn ineffective, they became more willing to experiment with civil disobedience.

Striking Pittston coal miners were the largest group to employ this approach. More than 4,000 of them and their supporters were arrested for sitting down in the road to block coal trucks. Their militant yet peaceful action played an important role in swinging the balance of power in their favor. In Minneapolis, hotel workers trained by peace activists sat down in the lobby of a hotel and brought a year-old contract conflict to a successful conclusion. Workers in other cities have also begun to experiment with this tactic, to train and prepare their members, to seek allies with experience, and break new ground.

This is the bottom line of the breakthroughs we have been exploring in this chapter. When we add together the new workers— service workers, white-collar professionals, women, immigrants, people of color—who are entering the labor movement in greater numbers than ever, the new kinds of organizations—participatory locals, family and support organizations, solidarity networks, labor-community coalitions—that have emerged, and the new strategies and tactics—social unionism, international solidarity, the organizing model, independent labor politics, corporate campaigns, civil disobedience, and inside strategies—that are being experimented with, we find the elements of a *new* labor movement. Though many activists may explain what they are doing as breathing new life into moribund organizations, trying out new tactics, or organizing the unorganized, the net result of all their actions is to lay the foundation for the labor movement's next historic leap.

It should not be surprising to us that the leaders of the existing labor movement are threatened by these developments. They expend more energy to stifle them than to fight on behalf of the workers whose dues pay their inflated salaries. They are committed to defending their own positions of privilege on the sinking ship of the existing labor movement. Our reading of history has prepared us to understand their action/inaction.

Social activists both within and outside the labor movement should not mistake the behavior of these "leaders" for the sentiments of the rank-and-file. This entire book has been intended to suggest that something else, something very significant is percolating beneath the surface, erupting here and there. This holds the promise of not simply a new stage in the historic development of the U.S. labor movement, but of a new broad-based social movement, one that can link the interests of the dispossessed and disfranchised in our country and across the world.

Chronology of the Hormel Conflict

July-November 1933. The Independent Union of All Workers (IUAW) is organized, conducts a sitdown strike, and wins recognition from the George A. Hormel & Company.

1933-1937. The IUAW spreads throughout Austin and to thirteen communities in Minnesota, Iowa, and Wisconsin.

April-August 1937. The IUAW dissolves itself, with most of its component parts affiliating with the Congress of Industrial Organizations (CIO). The Hormel local becomes part of the Packinghouse Workers Organizing Committee (PWOC).

1943. The CIO charters the United Packinghouse Workers of America and the Hormel local becomes Local 9.

1978. Hormel announces plans to build a new plant, threatening to build it outside Austin. Local P-9 agrees to major concessions to keep the plant in Austin: a five-year wage freeze and a no-strike contract; the placing of all premium pay in an escrow account lent to the company at 6 percent (which amounted to $12,000 per worker); the raising of work standards by 20 percent; and the phasing out of premium pay for exceeding standards. The company promises workers they will "never be worse off" in the new plant than they were in the old. Soon after the agreement is reached, the company closes the beef kill. Some workers transfer into the hog departments, some to the Hormel plant in Fort Dodge, Iowa (which would be closed itself in another four years), and some lose their jobs.

1979. Formation of United Food and Commercial Workers Union (UFCW) out of merger of United Packinghouse Workers, Amalgamated Meat Cutters, and Retail Clerks unions.

August 9, 1982. The new plant opens. Though more than 4,000 people had once worked in the old plant, no more than 1,750 would be employed in the new plant. Praised as "state of the art" by industry analysts, it includes the newest technology in hog slaughter and pork processing.

1982-1984. Hundreds of veteran workers quit after a taste of work in the new plant. By 1984, the majority of the workforce—more than 1,000—consists of new hires, most of whom have had no experience in the meatpacking industry.

December 1983. Jim Guyette, who has led rank-and-file opposition to concessions since the late 1970s, is elected president of Local P-9.

Spring-Summer 1984. Hormel gets the UFCW to reopen the Ottumwa contract for mid-term concessions. Soon afterwards, they announce their intentions to seek a 23 percent wage cut in all their plants, including Austin. Spouses of Hormel workers begin their support group.

October 1984. After a vote by the rank-and-file, Ray Rogers is invited to make a public presentation in Austin as to how to put pressure on a profitable company that seeks additional concessions from its workers. The response to the presentation is enthusiastic. That same month, a contract arbitrator rules that Hormel has the right to cut wages unilaterally. They do so (down to $8.25 an hour) and they deduct medical benefit "overpayments" from workers' shrunken paychecks. Some, particularly among the new hires—who have a high injury rate—can no longer make ends meet. The support group organizes a food shelf to help them out materially and the "tool box"—a peer counselling system—to help them out emotionally.

November-December 1984. Conflict between Local P-9 and the UFCW emerges. The international contends that Hormel is "the wrong target at the wrong time." They oppose hiring Rogers and they release a letter accusing the local of having "withdrawn from the Hormel chain" and having "broken solidarity" with the other Hormel locals. UFCW staffers distribute the letter to P-9ers, on company property and with company permission, while National Packinghouse Division director Lewie Anderson discusses it with the media. Hormel management reproduces the letter in a corporate publication.

December 9, 1984. Three thousand P-9ers, family members, and supporters march in Austin to protest wage cuts.

December 18, 1984. Ray Rogers is given fifteen minutes at the UFCW National Packinghouse Division meeting in Chicago to present a corporate campaign strategy to pressure Hormel to rescind the wage cuts. UFCW leaders reject Rogers' proposal and announce instead a nationwide campaign to unionize Con-Agra/Armour (which never gets off the ground).

January 17, 1985. P-9 rank-and-file vote to assess themselves $3 per week to hire Rogers and fund the corporate campaign against Hormel themselves.

January 29, 1985. Hormel holds its annual stockholders meeting outside of Austin for the first time in its 90-year history. A busload of P-9ers travel to Atlanta to attend and raise questions, and also to meet with rank-and-file workers at Hormel's partially unionized plant there.

February 1985. P-9er caravans visit other cities to meet other Hormel workers. They also come to metropolitan areas in the upper midwest to leaflet, explain their campaign, and seek support.

March 10, 1985. Guyette and Rogers speak to a public meeting at UAW Local 879 hall in St. Paul. The Twin Cities P-9 Support Committee is formed.

March 24, 1985. P-9 kicks off the "second phase" of its corporate campaign by zeroing in on First Bank Systems. Three thousand rally in Austin, with Twin Cities supporters given center stage.

April 12, 1985. Several hundred P-9ers attend First Bank stockholders meeting in St. Paul, where they demonstrate and raise questions about First Bank's relation with Hormel.

June 12, 1985. P-9 rank-and-file vote again to approve weekly $3 assessment for corporate campaign, since the UFCW challenged the propriety of the first vote in January.

June 28, 1985. Fifty local union activists from around the country meet with Rogers, Guyette, and Twin Cities supporters in St. Paul to discuss a nationwide network to resist concessions. The following day, they participate in a rally in Austin.

July 17, 1985. Hormel makes first—and only—contract offer, one month before expiration: a 150-page rewrite of the entire agreement. It includes: a retreat from plant-wide to departmental seniority; gutting the grievance procedure by limiting the scope of an arbitrator's authority; no commitment to dealing with safety problems; the elimination of both the "guaranteed annual wage" and the 52-week lay-off notice; concessions on wages and benefits; and an expiration date that would leave Austin out of sync with other Hormel locals.

August 9, 1985. UFCW President Bill Wynn grants P-9 strike sanction, but with explicit exclusion of roving pickets, product boycotts, and the corporate campaign. That night, P-9 rank-and-file votes 93 percent to 7 percent to reject the company's offer and go on strike.

August 17, 1985. The strike begins.

August 23, 1985. Hormel announces third-quarter profits up 83 percent over 1984.

August 31, 1985. Twin Cities P-9 Support Committee brings its first food caravan to Austin. Dozens of cars follow trucks carrying more than 100 tons of food. All participate in a rally in an outdoor park.

August-September 1985. P-9ers maintain nominal pickets at plant gates while focussing energies on outreach—caravans to other Hormel plants; mass demonstrations at First Bank facilities in Twin Cities and throughout the region; door-to-door leafletting in several communities.

September 24, 1985. An administrative law judge rules, on behalf of the regional National Labor Relations Board, that the corporate campaign against First Bank is an illegal secondary boycott under the provisions of the Taft-Hartley Act. U.S. District Court Judge Edward Devitt immediately issues an injunction which prohibits P-9's activities aimed at First Bank.

September 27, 1985. Minnesota State AFL-CIO annual convention meets in St. Paul. Leadership bans all P-9 literature on grounds it mentions First Bank and therefore runs afoul of Devitt's injunction. Leadership also denies Guyette an opportunity to address delegates, although he receives a standing ovation when he arrives. After an intensive lobbying effort by P-9ers and delegates who have been part of support activities, leadership allows a vaguely worded resolution calling for "support of all strikes in Minnesota" to come to a vote. It passes overwhelmingly.

October 19, 1985. P-9 discusses roving pickets, since Hormel has been able to shift production to some of its seven other plants as well as to FDL plants with which it has recently signed an exclusive marketing relationship. P-9 has already sent informational pickets to open communications with workers in these other locations. Since UFCW President Wynn explicitly forbade roving pickets in his strike sanction telegram, P-9 President Jim Guyette is instructed by rank-and-file vote to raise the issue with him again.

November 5, 1985. P-9 executive board meets with Wynn, National Packinghouse Division Director Lewie Anderson, and UFCW Region Director Joe Hansen in Chicago. Wynn promises to sanction roving pickets if Hansen reports that Hormel is not bargaining in good faith. Wynn and Guyette issue a joint statement, affirming that the strike still has official sanction and that P-9 and the international will work together. (In reality, Lewie Anderson had held secret strategy sessions with P-9 dissidents at a Twin Cities motel.)

November 1985. P-9 launches its "Adopt-a-Family" program to seek support from local unions across the country and to establish direct linkages between these locals and P-9 families. In the week before Thanksgiving, UFCW President Wynn writes to International Union officers of all AFL-CIO affiliates, urging them to discourage their locals from participating in this program on the grounds that the money will be given to Ray Rogers. Wynn recommends that union assistance to P-9 be channeled through the UFCW Region 13 office. (Long after the strike, P-9ers would learn from the UFCW's LM-2 form that the region office had *retained* $1.4 million which had been donated for P-9 and had charged it off against the paltry $45 a week strike benefits it had doled out.)

December 17, 1985. UFCW President Wynn refuses to sanction roving pickets. Hormel's seven other plants (five of which are under union contract) and the two unionized FDL plants will be allowed to continue to produce.

December 27-28, 1985. Under pressure from the UFCW, local politicians, and some of their own members, P-9 votes on the company's final offer (the July rewrite of the entire contract) again. The vote is held by secret ballot, with four local clergymen as the official vote counters. The result: rejection by a 2:1 margin.

January 3, 1986. The UFCW conducts its own mail ballot on the same offer. P-9ers reject it by the same margin. Hormel then announces that it will reopen the plant on Monday, January 13, and they invite P-9ers to return to work or face losing their jobs to "permanent replacements."

January 13, 1986. Amid much media fanfare, Hormel begins to take applications for "permanent replacements." Demonstrations at the plant gates pick up.

January 16, 1986. Wynn sends mailgram to Guyette, urging him to take yet another vote on the same proposal and warning him that P-9 is on the road to "mass suicide." The UFCW releases the mailgram to the media.

January 19, 1986. Huge solidarity rally held at St. Paul UAW Hall. "Labor Solidarity Brigade" of picket line volunteers enlists 450, who pledge to mark Martin Luther King Day by joining P-9's picket lines the next morning.

January 20, 1986. Hormel attempts to reopen with scabs, but Twin Cities supporters help shut the plant with a motor blockade. Some demonstrators also shut the corporate headquarters, locking in hundreds of corporate officials and white-collar workers at lunch time. Later that day, Governor Perpich announces that he is sending the National Guard to Austin to "protect public safety." Before sending in the Guard, Perpich consulted with state AFL-CIO president Dan Gustafson, Teamsters Joint Council Director Howard Fortier, and UAW Assistant Region Director Bob Killeen.)

January 21, 1986. Mobile demonstrators encircle the Guard and create a monster traffic jam at 4:00 AM. The plant fails to open for the day. That same day the UFCW International releases a 43-page "Fact Book on Local P-9/Austin, Minnesota" which attacks the elected leadership of P-9 and Ray Rogers, and even argues that Hormel has been reasonable in its bargaining.

January 23-24, 1986. P-9 executive board and Hormel management meet with "fact finder" appointed by the governor. No progress is made in these discussions. Meanwhile, support activities continue at a feverish pace. Thirty-five farmers arrive in Austin, having demonstrated at the state capitol for a moratorium on farm foreclosures. They lead a motorcade that encircles the plant and the Guard. Back at the state capitol, Twin Cities supporters and P-9 retirees begin a sit-in at the governor's office which will last several weeks.

January 24, 1986. The balance of power at the plant shifts again. When mobile pickets try to block the I-90 exit ramp that leads to the plant, state highway patrolmen break the windshields of their vehicles, pull them out, and arrest them in the sub-zero temperatures. Vehicles suffer damage as they are driven or towed away. The strikebreakers get through. For the next several days, the highway patrol limits access to a stretch of the interstate to people with passes identifying themselves as Hormel scabs. The Guard also restricts public access to numerous city streets. Signs appear: "Welcome to Austin, Poland." That night, Guyette appears on ABC-TV's "Nightline," with the UFCW's Lewie Anderson and U.S. Secretary of Labor Brock. Anderson argues that P-9 should be prepared to accept lower wages in order to establish a basic national wage in the industry. Guyette emphasizes the non-wage issues in the strike.

January 25, 1986. Five hundred supporters picket the governor's mansion in St. Paul, despite the minus-twenty-degree temperature, to demand that the Guard be pulled out of Austin.

January 26-27, 1986. P-9 begins to implement tactics without UFCW permission. On January 26, they issue a call for a nationwide boycott of Hormel products. On January 27, they send roving pickets to Hormel plants in Ottumwa, Iowa, and Fremont, Nebraska. In Ottumwa, more than 500 honor the picket lines and are fired. In Fremont, another 50 are fired.

January 28, 1986. Hormel holds annual stockholders meeting outside of Austin for the second year in a row, this time in Houston. They announce 1985 profits topped 1984's by 31 percent.

January 30, 1986. UFCW President Wynn telegrams other Hormel locals, warning them that the "Ayatollah of Austin [Ray Rogers] is making hostages of our members." Wynn urges local officers to prevent their rank-and-file from honoring P-9's pickets.

February 1, 1986. P-9's opponents claimed that the local union leadership was misrepresenting Hormel's contract offer to the rank-and-file. After sending in the National Guard, Governor Perpich appointed a "fact finder" to examine Hormel's proposal and prepare a "neutral" interpretation for the membership to consider. On the night of February 1, a rank-and-file meeting attended by 900 P-9ers voted overwhelmingly not to even consider the report from the governor's fact finder.

February 3, 1986. Guyette and Rogers cited for contempt of a restraining order, finded $250, and sentenced to fifteen days. Sentences stayed for six months.

February 4-5, 1986. Guyette and Rogers appear at AFL-CIO executive board meeting in Bal Harbour, Florida. President Lane Kirkland refuses to let them address the board. Wynn secures Kirkland's endorsement for a publication "UFCW Leadership Update: Special Report; UFCW Local P-9 Strikes Hormel: The

International Union's Perspective." Copies are circulated to delegates with Kirkland's blessings.

February 6, 1986. Twenty-seven protesters arrested when they attempt to perform a citizen's arrest on guardsmen who are blocking public streets. Rogers, among those arrested, is charged with "criminal syndicalism," a World War I law aimed at the repression of the IWW.

February 10, 1986. Hormel slaughters hogs for the first time since the strike began.

February 11, 1986. P-9 makes a new offer to the company— $10.05 an hour; some concessions on seniority language; but the rehiring of everyone who has been replaced or fired in Austin, Ottumwa, and Fremont. Hormel rejects the offer.

February 12, 1986. Hormel claims to have hired a full workforce in Austin—650 "permanent replacements" and 450 P-9ers who have crossed their own picket lines. They also announce their intention to close the kill and cut operation in Ottumwa.

February 13, 1986. UFCW executive board issues statement, "Local P-9 Strike Against Hormel," which condemns the strike and attacks Rogers personally as a "union buster."

February 15, 1986. Six thousand rally in Austin in response to a nationwide call.

February 21, 1986. National Guard withdraw from the plant. Several hundred high school students, members of "P-9: The Future Generation," walk out of school and demonstrate at the plant gates. P-9 pulls pickets at Ottumwa. "Terminated" workers march on the plant and demand their jobs back. Gates are locked in their faces.

March 10, 1986. One hundred and twelve P-9ers and supporters are arrested in civil disobedience at corporate headquarters.

March 14, 1986. Wynn sends telegram to P-9 members, ordering an immediate and unconditional return to work. He sends a letter to each P-9er, which includes a stamped envelope addressed to the Hormel personnel manager. Wynn also promises "post-strike assistance" checks to those who follow his orders.

March 16, 1986. P-9 rank-and-file meet; 800 in attendance. They vote overwhelmingly to continue the strike. Membership also votes to bring a lawsuit against the UFCW for "malicious interference" with the strike. That same evening, Twin Cities supporters, led by folksinger Larry Long, hold a "Boycott Hormel" concert at the UAW Hall. Professional quality cassette tapes ("Boycott Hormel") and videotapes ("We're Not Gonna Take It") now join hats, buttons, stickers, and T-shirts in publicizing the struggle against Hormel.

March 23, 1986. Benefit basketball game pits team of P-9ers vs. UAW 879, at Pacelli High School in Austin.

March 26, 1986. Dr. Kevin O'Dell, Pacelli principal, fired by Catholic Board of Education. Though they denied that O'Dell's willingness to rent the school gym to Local P-9 was the cause of his dismissal, no other substantive explanation was ever offered. This was but one example of how P-9 was denied access to community institutions in its efforts to defend itself.

April 1-11, 1986. Mounting demonstrations at the plant gates in Austin, as supporters from across the country stream in for a major rally. On April 5, food caravans organized by support committees in the Twin Cities, Madison, and Milwaukee converge on Austin, delivering more than 200 tons of food.

April 11, 1986. Seventeen arrested on felony riot charges at plant gates after police and county sheriffs tear-gas demonstrators. Ray Rogers is arrested and charged with "aiding and abetting" a riot for having mailed posters and flyers inviting people to come to Austin; a warrant with the same charges is issued for Jim Guyette.

April 12, 1986. Six thousand supporters from across the country march and demonstrate solidarity with P-9.

April 13, 1986. Jesse Jackson arrives in Austin, prays with the workers in prison, and urges P-9ers to "keep their eyes on the prize": the return of their jobs with dignity.

April 14-16, 1986. UFCW holds trusteeship hearing in Minneapolis. Not only is the hearing closed to the public, but with most of the 50 seats occupied by UFCW staffers, few P-9ers can even attend. The examiner, a local official from Texas, restricts testimony and evidence to one question only: Did P-9 disobey the UFCW order on March 14 to call off the strike?

April 23, 1986. U.S. District Judge Edward Devitt issues a new federal injunction, at the request of the NLRB, prohibiting P-9ers from taking pictures of scabs crossing the picket line.

May 8, 1986. The UFCW announces it has taken over Local P-9 through trusteeship.

May 9, 1986. The UFCW appears before Judge Devitt and requests and receives a restraining order halting P-9's control over its own funds.

May 17, 1986. "National Boycott Day" is held in dozens of cities around the country.

May 23, 1986. UFCW Trustee Joe Hansen informs Hormel that Local P-9 is making an "unconditional offer" of a return to work.

June 2-5, 1986. Armed with court orders from Judge Devitt, UFCW Region Director Joe Hansen takes over P-9 and places two deputy trustees in charge. (Both had been local officers elsewhere in the UFCW and had been voted out of office by their own members for their advocacy of granting concessions. One later took a position in personnel management at Hormel's FDL subsidiary.) Trustees tell P-9ers they must cease the boycott and can no longer speak publicly about their struggle. They demand that bumper stickers be taken off vehicles and that buttons not be worn. (Generally, they are ignored.) They also seize P-9 bank accounts, have mail redirected to them, fire P-9's two long-term secretaries, and evict P-9 from its offices in the Austin Labor Center. (They will also challenge the applications of P-9's full-time officers for unemployment benefits, arguing that they were fired "for cause.")

June 6, 1986. UFCW mails letter to local unions throughout the United States urging the purchase of Hormel products, "made by union brothers and sisters, earning the best wages and benefits in the industry." The mailing includes a sticker to place inside vending machines, so it can't be removed, reading: "Hormel products are union-made." (The boycott had been most successful in the lunchrooms of unionized workplaces.)

June 9, 1986. UFCW President Wynn mails letter to union officials across the United States, urging them not to contribute to P-9's legal fund (for the eighteen facing felony charges and the more than 200 facing misdemeanor charges), on grounds that the money will be used to sue the international union.

June 20, 1986. In response to P-9's charges that the Hormel Foundation, officially set up by Jay Hormel's family "in the best interest of the community of Austin," was damaging the community and manipulating local charities and social services against the strikers, Minnesota Attorney General Skip Humphrey issued a report finding no legal violations in the Foundation's behavior.

June 22-28, 1986. P-9ers and supporters organize "Solidarity City." Hundreds of supporters from around the country come to Austin, pitch tents, and participate in demonstrations, workshops, and discussions. In addition to trade unionists, participants include welfare activists, peace activists, college students, Rainbow Coalition promoters, and Native Americans. No institution in Austin will rent space, so tents are pitched on a retiree's land outside town. He is later fired from his job at the Austin YMCA (which is heavily subsidized by the Hormel Foundation). Fifteen hundred march and rally on June 28.

July 3, 1986. Armed with yet another ruling from Judge Devitt, the UFCW trustees evict the United Support Group and the P-9 Retirees organization from the Austin Labor Center. The two groups rent other space and move.

July 7, 1986. Organized as the "North American Meat Packers Union," some P-9ers file a "recertification" petition to challenge the UFCW. They had already circulated one petition as "Original P-9," but the NLRB ruled they could not use this name.

September 13, 1986. UFCW Region Director Hansen announces that a new Hormel-UFCW contract has been ratified and signs it. In essence, it follows the company's rewrite of the entire agreement, from seniority to arbitration, with an expiration date out of sync with most other Hormel plants.

September 26, 1986. Hansen writes all P-9ers that the new contract prohibits boycott activity, and that under its terms, they can be stricken from the recall list for continuing to promote the boycott of Hormel products.

October 8, 1986. Trustees sandblast strike mural on outside wall of Austin Labor Center, despite protests from hundreds of artists around the country and the unwillingness of Austin building trades workers to do the job.

October 11, 1986. United Support Group holds its second anniversary party.

November 6, 1986. Hormel and UFCW Trustee Joe Hansen draw up a formal strike settlement agreement.

November 20, 1986. Twin Cities supporters organize fundraiser concert at Minneapolis' Orchestra Hall, featuring Arlo Guthrie, Holly Near, John McCutcheon, and Larry Long. Nearly 2,000 attend, representing virtually every oppositional movement in the upper midwest.

December 5, 1986. Hormel acquires Jenni-O Turkey, continuing their pattern of diversifying and acquiring other product names (FDL-Dubuque; New Traditions; Top Shelf; Chicken by George).

March 14, 1987. More than 1,000 P-9ers and supporters rally in Austin to "turn up the heat on Hormel."

May 1-3, 1987. About 60 activists attend Mid-America Conference of Rank-and-file Packinghouse Workers in Austin. They adopt a "Packinghouse Workers' Bill of Rights."

July 3-5, 1987. P-9ers and supporters organize "Cram Your Spam" Days as a counter-activity to Austin Chamber of Commerce's turning annual Cedar River Days into "Spam Days" to mark the 50th anniversary of the creation of Spam. Second annual "Tent City" held in conjunction with "Cram Your Spam" Days. The lawn of P-9 executive board member Skinny Weis in the center of town is covered with hundreds of white crosses, each bearing the name of a replaced P-9er.

July 15, 1987. UFCW ends trusteeship over what they now call "Local 9." John Morrison and John Anker, who conspired with Lewie Anderson and then crossed the picket line, are elected secretary-treasurer and president of the local. Morrison had appeared at "Spam Days" wearing a shiny new "SPAM" T-shirt that was given out free by Hormel. (Morrison is also the "star" of *American Dream,* as filmmaker Barbara Koppel featured his agonies about crossing the picket line.)

1988-1989. Hormel continues restructuring. They sell the Ottumwa plant to Excell, who hires an almost entirely new workforce. They close the hog kill and cut in their brand-new Austin plant, later sub-contracting it out to a new company which, under the UFCW contract, pays workers $6.50 an hour. The scab officers of Local 9 are routinely shunned at UFCW Region 13 and Minnesota State AFL-CIO conventions. In February 1989, National Packinghouse Division Direction Lewie Anderson is fired by President Wynn. Still holding the position of vice president, he begins to organize a "reform" movement, called "REAP" (for research, education, advocacy, and people). Hundreds of P-9ers are stricken from the recall list for boycott activity. Hormel begins to call back some of the P-9ers in the summer of 1989, after they and UFCW Local 9 renegotiate the strike settlement agreement to take away seniority for time served on the recall list, giving scabs and crossovers super-seniority. By the summer of 1992, more than 300 P-9ers have returned to work.

1980-1990. Average real take-home wages in the U.S. meatpacking industry fell by 44 percent. Meanwhile, Hormel Chief Executive Officer Richard Knowlton's annual salary, plus stock options, rose from $238,000 to more than $3,000,000.

Selected Bibliography

Aronowitz, Stanley, *False Promises* (Chapel Hill, NC: Duke Univ. Press, 1987).

Aronowitz, Stanley, *Working-Class Hero* (NY: Adama Publishers, 1984).

Benson, Herman, *Democratic Rights for Union Members* (New York: Association for Union Democracy, 1979).

Bluestone, Barry and Bennett Harrison, *The Deindustrialization of America* (NY: Basic Books, 1984).

Bluestone, Barry and Bennett Harrison, *The Great U-Turn* (NY: Basic Books, 1988).

Brecher, Jeremy and Tim Costello, eds., *Building Bridges: The Emerging Grassroots Coalition of Labor and Community* (NY: Monthly Review, 1990).

Brecher, Jeremy, *Strike!* (Boston, MA: South End Press, 1977).

Davis, Mike, *Prisoners of the American Dream* (NY: Verso, 1986).

Fantasia, Rick, *Cultures of Solidarity* (Berkeley: Univ. of California Press, 1988).

Ferguson, Thomas and Joel Rogers, *Right Turn: The Decline of the Democrats and the Future of American Politics* (NY: Hill and Wang, 1986).

Fitz, Don & Dave Roediger, eds., *Within the Shell of the Old* (Chicago: C.H. Kerr, 1989).

Friedman, Sam, *Teamster Rank & File* (NY: Columbia Univ. Press, 1982).

Garson, Barbara, *The Electronic Sweatshop* (NY: Viking, 1989).

Gilpin, Toni et al, *On Strike for Respect: The Clerical and Technical Workers' Strike at Yale University, 1984-85* (Chicago: C.H. Kerr, 1988).

Goldfield, Michael, *The Decline of Organized Labor in the United States* (Chicago: Univ of Chicago Press, 1987).

Green, Hardy, *On Strike at Hormel* (Philadelphia: Temple University Press, 1990).

Hall, Burton, ed., *Autocracy and Insurgency in Organized Labor* (New Brunswick, NJ: Transaction Publishers, 1972).

Hayes, Dennis, *Behind the Silicon Curtain* (Boston, MA: South End Press, 1989).

Horowitz, Roger, "From UPWA to UFCW: Meatpacker Unionism Gutted," *Against the Current,* 6, November-December 1986.

Howard, Robert, *Brave New Workplace* (NY: Viking, 1986).

Kochan, Thomas, ed., *Challenges and Choices Facing American Labor* (Cambridge, MA: Massachusetts Institute of Technology, 1985).

LaBotz, Dan, *Rank & File Rebellion: Teamsters for a Democratic Union* (NY: Verso, 1990).

LaBotz, Dan, *A Troublemaker's Handbook* (Detroit, MI: Labor Notes, 1991).

Lynd, Staughton, *Labor Law for the Rank & Filer* (San Pedro, CA: Singlejack, 1978).

Lynd, Alice & Staughton, eds., *Rank & File* (NY: Monthly Review, 1988).

Lynd, Staughton, *The Fight Against Shutdowns* (San Pedro, CA: Singlejack, 1982).

Lynd, Staughton, *Solidarity Unionism* (Chicago: C.H. Kerr, 1992).

Mann, Eric, *Taking on General Motors* (Los Angles, CA: Univ. of California, 1987).

Moody, Kim, *An Injury to All* (NY: Verso, 1988).

Noble, David, *Forces of Production* (NY: Oxford University Press, 1986).

Parker, Mike, *Inside the Circle* (Boston, MA: South End Press, 1985).

Perry, Charles, *Union Corporate Campaigns* (Philadelphia, PA: Univ. of Philadelphia, 1987).

Schatz, Ronald, *The Electrical Workers* (Urbana, IL: Univ. of Illinois, 1983).

Schor, Juliet, *The Overworked American* (NY: Basic Books, 1992).

Serrin, William, *The Company and the Union* (NY: Knopf, 1972).

Shaiken, Harley, *Work Transformed* (NY: Free Press, 1984).

Shostak, Arthur and David Skocik, *The Air Traffic Controllers' Controversy* (NY: Human Sciences Press, 1986).

Slaughter, Jane, *Concessions and How to Beat Them* (Detroit, MI: Labor Notes, 1983).

Slaughter, Jane and Mike Parker, *Choosing Sides: Unions and the Team Concept* (Boston, MA: South End Press, 1985).

Index

use of civil disobedience by, 65,
66-67, 120
see also Hormel Strike
Long, Larry, 66, 67, 69, 120, 123

M

McCutcheon, John, 69, 123
Machinists' Union (International
Association of Machinists), 69, 71
"management prerogatives," 18-19
Mazzocchi, Tony, 108, 109
media, 77-78, 88
Metsa, Paul, 11
Mid-America Conference of
Rank-and-File Packinghouse Workers,
124
Minneapolis Citizens Alliance, 38
Minnesota AFL-CIO, 70, 71, 82, 116
Minnesota Fair Trade Coalition, 106
Minnesota Nurses Association, 100
Minnesota State Federation of Labor
(AFL-CIO), 70-71. *See also* Gustafson,
Dan
mission statements, 108
Moody, Kim, 24-25, 26
Morrell company, 50
Morris, David, 14
Morrison, John, 57, 86, 124
"movement culture," 17, 55, 58
Mower County Food Shelf, 77
Mower County Mental Health Clinic, 77
Msane, Amon, 70
Myre, Helmer, 38, 39, 40

N

"National Boycott Day," 122
National Guard, 15, 69, 77, 120
use of, to break Hormel Strike, 67, 77,
79-80, 118-119
National Labor Relations Act (Wagner
Act), 10, 17
National Labor Relations Board (NLRB),
10, 11, 22, 58, 116
National Lawyers Guild, 84

National Packinghouse Committee, 57
"National Rank-and-file Against
Concessions" (NRFAC), 72
Near, Holly, 69, 123
Nilson, Carl, 33, 35, 37, 38, 41
Nilson, Marian, 33
North American Free Trade Agreement,
106-107
North American Meat Packers Union
(NAMPU), 86, 123
Northern States Power (NSP), 49
Nyberg, Charles, 83

O

O'Dell, Kevin, 121
Olsen, Tillie, 68
Olson, Floyd, 31, 40
On Strike for Respect (Gilpin), 102
"organizing model," 107-108, 110
Oscar Mayer company, 54
Ottumwa, Iowa plant, 52, 67, 69, 83, 120,
124

P

P-9. *See* Local P-9
"P-9: The Future Generation," 62, 120
"P-10," 57-83
Packinghouse Workers of America, 113
Packinghouse Workers Organizing
Committee (PWOC), 41, 113
"pattern" agreements, 18
Peltier, Leonard, 70
"permanent replacements," 13-14, 75,
110, 117, 120
in Hormel Strike, 80, 117. *See also*
scabs
Perpich, Rudy, 67, 79-80, 118, 119
Peterson, Norman "Injunction," 39
Phelps Dodge strike, 13
pickets, roving, 67, 76, 83, 116-117
Pittston strike, 81, 104, 111
pledge cards, 108

About South End Press

South End Press is a nonprofit, collectively-run book publisher with over 175 titles in print. Since our founding in 1977, we have tried to meet the needs of readers who are exploring, or are already committed to, the politics of radical social change.

Our goal is to publish books that encourage critical thinking and constructive action on the key political, cultural, social, economic, and ecological issues shaping life in the United States and in the world. In this way, we hope to give expression to a wide diversity of democratic social movements and to provide an alternative to the products of corporate publishing.

Through the Institute for Social and Cultural Change, South End Press works with other political media projects—*Z Magazine;* Speak Out!, a speakers bureau; the Publishers Support Project; and the New Liberation News Service—to expand access to information and critical analysis. If you would like a free catalog of South End Press books or information about our membership program—which offers two free books and a 40% discount on all titles—please write to us at South End Press, 116 Saint Botolph Street, Boston, MA 02115.

Other SEP titles of interest

Mask of Democracy
Labor Suppression in Mexico Today
Dan La Botz

Workers of the World Undermined
American Labor's Role in U.S. Foreign Policy
Beth Sims

Labor Law Handbook
Michael Yates

Strike!
A History of the American Workers' Movement
Jeremy Brecher